OVERVIEW

Overview

Using inefficient procedures is like digging a 200-foot wide hole for a 100-foot wide house. You'll have wasted a great deal of effort on something you don't really need. Your organization must make shrewd investments in its precious time, money, and effort. You need flexible, intelligent strategies to evolve and prosper in a competitive global market.

Lean is a methodology that incorporates a powerful set of tools and techniques designed to maximize customer value while constantly working to reduce waste. It focuses on improving overall efficiency, quality, and customer satisfaction.

Because of its ability to improve customer satisfaction and deliver bottom-line financial gains, Lean is a preferred strategic choice for many organizations. This course introduces you to the basic principles of Lean, which will help you create more efficient processes and get you on the road to successful operations management.

Sorin Dumitrascu

This course also outlines the five-step process for implementing Lean. By learning how to implement Lean in your organization, you can reduce the costs of developing your company's product, increase production efficiency, and improve safety, quality, and performance levels. Finally, the course explains how Lean integrates with the Six Sigma production management system. Using this hybrid approach enables you to minimize process and product defects, and to identify and resolve pervasive problems.

Today's markets are very competitive and customers insist on the best quality products for their money. This means that businesses must actively pursue perfection to keep their customers and to retain their market share. Pursuing perfection and excellent quality are important principles of Lean thinking. Continuous improvement, the elimination of waste, and striving toward zero defects all help organizations attract and keep customers, and so increase their profitability.

This course introduces four Lean tools organizations use to strive for perfection and improve quality – 5S, Hoshin Kanri, jidoka and poka yoke, and standard work. As you work through this course, you'll find out what these tools are, their purpose, and how the tools are used. You should then be able to recognize how the tools may be used in your own organization.

The course provides examples of how the Lean tools can be applied in both manufacturing and service organizations. It will help you assess your own organization's needs and determine how you can apply the tools to perfect what you offer.

How can you make your organization more efficient? The simplest way is to eliminate waste from your processes. This waste can be caused by many factors, such as untidy workspaces and surplus inventory. Or it might be caused by inefficient distribution of work. Using Lean tools, you can make your processes smoother and your workspaces tidier.

To implement a Lean solution, you must know what tools and techniques are available, and which ones would best help you. You have to select the best blend of Lean techniques for your organization. You can use a number of Lean techniques to make your organization run more smoothly. These include the visual workplace, just-in-time, kanban, and line balancing.

The visual workplace uses signs and other visual cues to convey information quickly. The visual cues include work instructions, process flow diagrams, and status boards.

Just-in-time ensures that you have exactly the right amount of supplies needed at any time. This helps to reduce surplus inventory. Kanban cards are triggers that alert the team to send more parts or supplies. The parts are then "pulled" into the system, based on demand. Line balancing results in the even distribution of work among workers. No workers are overburdened, and no workers are left idle. Using the Lean techniques outlined in this course will help you to develop strategies for improving flow and pull in your organization.

For your business to be the best it can be, you need to eliminate what doesn't work and improve what does. In Lean thinking, this translates to reducing or eliminating waste and improving the flow of production. This course introduces approaches you can use to do just that, in both the manufacturing and service environments.

Before you can reduce waste, you need to recognize where and how it's occurring. In this course, you'll learn how to do this by determining which of your company's activities add value and which don't. Once you've categorized activities, you can search for ways to eliminate those that don't add value or, if they're required, to minimize the resources spent on them. And for activities that do add value, you can find ways to optimize this value.

Next you'll learn about the different forms of waste that you find in a business and the typical causes of each type of waste. You'll also learn various strategies for minimizing or eliminating each of the waste types.

This course also explains the concept of continuous flow, which depends on the removal of obstacles and bottlenecks in work processes. You'll learn how to balance work processes to enhance flow, with the aim of producing what's needed, when it's needed, in the quantities required. Using the strategies outlined in this course can improve the efficiency of your business, moving its processes closer to perfection.

Suppose on your first day of work, your boss tells you too many defects have crept into the company's product. She then asks for your input on how to solve the problem. But without knowing how the company's current processes work, it's unlikely you'll have useful suggestions. To improve processes, you first need to understand them.

To understand how something works, you need to observe it, noting how it fits into a larger pattern. Creating a visual representation of the material and information flow that leads to the creation of a product or service can help. This is called value stream mapping.

With a value stream map, you can search for flaws, work out why problems exist, and plan how to eliminate them. This course teaches you how to use value stream mapping as a tool for improving an organization's processes and making them more efficient. You'll learn how to create a current-state value stream map, analyze the current state, and then create a future-state map.

Create a current-state map

The course provides an overview of the steps involved in creating a current-state map and of the symbols typically used in this type of map.

Analyze current state

The current-state map provides a big-picture view of a targeted process. This makes it easier to identify where waste is occurring and why.

Create a future-state map

You'll learn how to create a future-state value stream map. This involves searching for and then recording opportunities to balance the production line, create pull, and eliminate sources of waste.

In this course, you'll learn how value stream mapping can be used, in both manufacturing and service industries. It will prove a valuable tool you can use to improve efficiency and eliminate waste, ultimately boosting both customer satisfaction and an organization's profits.

Despite the relative simplicity of many Lean tools, a majority of attempts to adopt Lean in an organization fail. Why does this happen? The chief cause of failure to convert to a Lean enterprise is lack of awareness that it requires a culture change, rather than simply a change in tools. Transformation to a Lean enterprise calls for a complete change in the way everyone in the organization thinks about work, as well as slight work modifications.

Flirting with Lean tools won't create a meaningful or lasting improvement in an organization. To truly embrace and integrate Lean principles, an organization has to make a long-term commitment to the change. It also has to change its culture. All employees need to practice applying Lean concepts daily, until Lean thinking becomes an accepted and routine part of how they think and behave. It requires a cultural change.

A permanent shift to the Lean philosophy can occur only from a continuous improvement philosophy. When this occurs, organizational and customer benefits will be realized. So you need to encourage and practice continuous improvement daily to truly integrate the shift in culture. This course provides a guide to the benefits and characteristics of a Lean culture. It provides tips and strategies for facilitating a culture change through the use of kaizen. And it provides a detailed guide on how to plan for and implement a kaizen event in your organization.

CHAPTER I - INTRODUCTION TO LEAN FOR SERVICE AND MANUFACTURING

CHAPTER I - Introduction to Lean for Service and Manufacturing
  SECTION 1 - Basic Principles of Lean
  SECTION 2 - The Five Steps to Lean
  SECTION 3 - Integrating Lean and Six Sigma

SECTION 1 - BASIC PRINCIPLES OF LEAN

SECTION 1 - Basic Principles of Lean

Lean is a production management methodology that incorporates four main principles – eliminating waste, achieving flow in the value stream, continuous improvement, and maintaining an efficient workplace. Implementing these principles helps manufacturing, service, transaction, and retail industries to work more efficiently and cost effectively, while improving quality and delivery speeds.

ELIMINATION OF WASTE

Elimination of waste

In the 1950's, Toyota was on the verge of bankruptcy. Taiichi Ohno, the assembly manager, was tasked with turning the company around. Based on his observations of the Ford factory and of supermarket replenishment systems, Ohno developed a new philosophy and practice – called Lean. This dramatically changed the situation for Toyota, turning it into one of the most profitable and productive organizations in the industry.

Since its beginnings in the automotive industry, Lean has been embraced globally in manufacturing, service, and retail industries. And the results have been staggering.

By adopting Lean practices, businesses are able to produce higher quality products faster, more cheaply, and more reliably. They create what their customers need using less inventory, space, energy, and time.

By learning Lean principles and applying them in your organization, you can increase safety, capacity, yield, performance, quality, and the level of team integration. All of this ultimately boosts profitability.

For example, a hospital group's adoption of Lean saved $6 million in planned capital investment, freed 13,000 square feet of space, cut inventory costs by $360,000, reduced staff walking distances by 34 miles a day, and improved patient satisfaction.

Question

What do you think learning the basic Lean principles can enable you to do?

Options:

1. Reduce the time taken and cost to develop your company's product
2. Improve work safety, product quality, and performance levels
3. Reduce the number of employees that your company hires
4. Reduce team work and increase individual input

Answer:

Option 1: This option is correct. Lean reduces waste and streamlines processes, helping organizations to work smarter. This results in far shorter cycle times in product development and reduces costs.

Option 2: This is a correct option. By improving work practices and ensuring high-quality products, you boost employee performance and customer satisfaction.

Option 3: This is an incorrect option. Reduction in the number of employees is a strategic decision usually taken at the corporate level and is beyond the scope of Lean implementation in an organization.

Option 4: This option is incorrect. In fact, Lean focuses on creating teams in which all employees work together to reduce waste and improve quality.

So what was Taiichi Ohno's secret? The approach he developed can be broken down into four main principles – eliminating waste, achieving flow in the value stream, continuous improvement, and maintaining an efficient workplace.

In a Lean workplace, "waste" is any activity that doesn't add value for a customer. If a customer is willing to pay for an activity or feature, it has value. Only a small fraction of business activities typically adds value for customers. Often 50% or more of a business's activities are considered waste.

A primary cause of waste is information deficits. Employees may lack the knowledge they need to do their jobs efficiently and effectively. As a result, they may waste valuable time and effort searching for, asking for, waiting for, retrieving, or reworking items. In addition to information deficits, common causes of waste include overstocking raw material, overproducing, and using poor processes and work practices.

Overstocking raw material

If you purchase more wood than is required to manufacture furniture, you need to pay to transport and store the wood. It takes time and money to retrieve the wood from storage, and if any wood is damaged, you have to pay to dispose of it.

Similarly, if you purchase a large number of paper manuals for call center staff to refer to, they take up floor space and must be shelved on bookcases. It takes staff time and effort to find the correct manuals, and once they're obsolete or damaged, you have to replace them.

Overproducing

Overproducing finished goods is another significant cause of waste. Manufacturing, transporting, storing, and maintaining surplus goods all add to costs, without increasing value for customers.

Overproduction may also occur In the service industry. For example, customers may receive unwanted – or "surplus" – information or services. Why mail product information booklets that are simply discarded without being read? This wastes customers' time and the time and resources of the organization.

Using poor processes and work practices

Poor processes and work practices waste time, money, and labor. They can also cause employees to become frustrated and make mistakes, which could threaten their safety.

Suppose you have a government contract to repair roads and you use too many people and too much equipment for the task. This unnecessarily increases equipment storage and maintenance costs. Also, workers may become frustrated or distracted on the roads and this could endanger their safety.

Question

Which are examples of waste?

Options:

1. Waiting for a coworker to complete her work before you can do yours

2. Transporting parts and materials around the plant

3. Conducting market research to find out what your customers want

4. Upgrading software functionality to meet new customer demands

Answer:

Lean for Business Organizations

Waiting for coworkers and transporting stock to warehouses unnecessarily are examples of waste. Discovering and meeting customer demands are activities that add value for customers, so they aren't wasteful.

VALUE FLOW AND KAIZEN

Value flow and kaizen

The second Lean principle is achieving perfect flow in your organization's value stream. Value is defined as what a customer wants and is willing to pay for. The value stream is all the tasks, actions, and information used to create a deliverable and get it to the customer.

Achieving perfect flow requires the removal of all obstacles and waste – known as "muda" – from the value stream. This will optimize the flow of production and delivery to the customer.

Assessing your organization's value stream can help you identify waste and add value to processes. This applies for both manufacturing and service organizations.

Manufacturing

Value-added activities for an automobile manufacturer include design, manufacture, and safety testing of vehicles. The current value stream should also show all communications and quality controls used.

Typical barriers include batch jobs and queues, or waiting. You can remove obstacles to flow by reducing work batches so that smaller jobs are processed and by using cross-functional teams to work project by project.

Service

Value-added activities for a hospital include diagnosing, treating, and providing aftercare. The current value stream should also show the use of communications and quality controls, and the type of information that's required.

Each value-added activity needs to be analyzed to discover smarter and more efficient ways of performing them. Activities that aren't value-added need to be eliminated or redesigned to add value to the process.

For example, micromanagement causes waiting time and low morale, because clear processes aren't defined and workers don't have the responsibility to do their work.

Perfecting the value stream is tied to the principle of continuous improvement, known as kaizen. This principle requires everyone to assess and improve processes and practices repeatedly, to streamline them and reduce waste. So it involves ongoing, incremental change with the aim of better meeting customer demand.

Question

How often are improvements made in your organization?

Options:

1. Daily
2. Monthly
3. Yearly

Answer:

Option 1: Your organization is already working with the principle of kaizen. If employees at all levels in their areas of expertise generate these changes, and if the changes are designed to remove waste and meet customer demands, the principle is intact.

Option 2: Intermittent changes can be disruptive and fail to deal with problems as they arise. Finding out more about how to implement kaizen in your organization will help you to streamline processes and practices.

Option 3: Large intermittent changes can be disruptive and fail to deal with problems as they arise. Finding out more about how to implement kaizen in your organization will help you to streamline processes and practices.

It's important to re-evaluate production processes continually. Even if a process appears to work well, it doesn't mean that it's perfect – there's always room for improvement.

EFFICIENT WORKPLACE

Efficient workplace

The fourth Lean principle is maintaining an efficient workplace to prevent workers from wasting time and effort searching for the tools or components they need to do their jobs. Lean provides a five-step process known as 5S to create a disciplined, clean, and well-ordered work environment.

The first step in the 5S process is called "Seiri", which means Sort. The second is "Seiton" – or Set in place. The third step is "Seiso", which means Shine. The fourth is "Seiketsu" – or Standardize, and the final step is "Shitsuke", which means Sustain.

Sort

The first step requires that you tidy and sort through all items in the work area, removing unnecessary items.

Set in place

The second step requires that you set the remaining items in place so that their positioning makes ergonomic sense. This removes the need for unnecessary motion.

Shine

The third step involves cleaning and tidying, and returning anything that has been moved to its correct place. All employees should perform this step daily at the ends of their shifts.

Standardize

The fourth step is to standardize work processes in each workspace. It may also involve developing visual aids to outline these processes. This step helps employees to work consistently and ensures they know what's expected of them.

Sustain

The final step is to sustain the order created and to integrate 5S practice into daily work. This involves maintaining standards, educating employees, and communicating what's needed to keep the work area and processes as ergonomic as possible.

If you ever visit a well-organized fire station, you'll be able to witness 5S at work. Uniforms are within easy grasp of the firefighters, equipment is clearly labeled, trucks are kept clean and shiny, and the pole minimizes the time and effort required to move from the top floor to the ground floor, where the fire trucks are waiting.

This attention to workspace design means that firefighters don't waste time when called out in emergencies.

Question

Now review what you've learned about Lean so far.
What are the basic Lean principles?

Options:

1. Eliminating waste
2. Continuously improving processes

3. Improving speed and quality through a smoothly flowing value stream
4. Creating and maintaining an efficient workspace
5. Eliminating product errors
6. Using a top-down approach for problem solving

Answer:

Option 1: This option is correct. Lean classifies anything that doesn't add value, or that a customer would be unwilling to pay for, as waste. Lean prioritizes identifying and eliminating this waste.

Option 2: This is a correct option. A Lean approach involves continuous improvement, or kaizen. It requires everyone in an organization to assess and improve processes continually.

Option 3: This option is correct. The value stream comprises all the tasks, actions, and information used to create a deliverable and get it to customers. Lean requires the removal of all waste and obstacles that impede the flow of value to the customer.

Option 4: This is a correct option. A Lean approach includes setting up and maintaining a process-oriented, uncluttered workspace, as well as standardized work processes.

Option 5: This option is incorrect. Lean focuses on eliminating waste rather than specifically on reducing product defects.

Option 6: This is an incorrect option. With Lean, everyone in an organization is expected to assess and improve processes. It's the responsibility of all employees – not just of managers – to address problems.

INDUSTRY USES

Industry uses

Although Lean began in the manufacturing industry, it has also been successfully adopted by a range of service industries, including those in the banking, healthcare, and retail sectors.

The basic principles of Lean apply across all industries. For example, you can apply the following steps, no matter what your organization does:
- understand your customers' requirements,
- map your organization's value stream,
- identify and eliminate waste,
- calculate the allowed time to produce a single product to match customer demand – which is known as takt time,
- implement kaizen, and implement 5S in your workspace.

Lean tools and principles can be used in the manufacturing industry. Many of these tools and principles can also be used in non-manufacturing and service industries, such as banking, healthcare and retail.

Some key tools and strategies for implementing Lean in the manufacturing environment include creating work modules, just-in-time – or JIT – production, just-enough inventory, and standardization.

Work modules

Production work should be organized into product groups in a clockwise layout that provides all the necessary equipment to manufacture the product or part. Teams working within this area should have the necessary skills and knowledge to use, maintain, and repair the equipment they work with.

JIT production

JIT production works on a "pull" system where products or parts are created or ordered as they are needed.

For example, a factory worker who bolts metal sheets can use the "two-bin" system, where she has two containers holding 50 bolts each. When the first container empties, it's sent to be replenished, while she continues to use the bolts in the second container.

Another useful system is the kanban-card method, where information such as part number and location are updated as the card travels with the inventory. Each card triggers inventory replacement once the part is consumed.

Just-enough inventory

Manufacturers implement Lean by reducing inventory as much as possible. You calculate the minimum inventory required and keep that where workers can use it.

If it's impossible to work like this, very small amounts of inventory should be stored and these should be kept and transported as efficiently as possible.

Standardization

Even though you may manufacture a variety of goods, notice where the processes and tasks are similar and standardize these. Unique tasks and processes should be compartmentalized.

For example, suppose your company creates custom furniture. Tasks that may be standardized include design processes, cutting sections of wood, sanding, polishing, creating joins, and transporting completed pieces.

Service industries also include airlines, IT services, shipping, education and training, repair and maintenance, food and hospitality, and many governmental agencies.

To implement Lean within a service industry, services should be viewed as products. To meet customer needs, they should be designed and generated using specific processes.

The second feature of implementing Lean in the service industry is to focus on increasing the speed and quality of processes and service delivery.

Continuously improving processes by eliminating waste from the value flow and maintaining an efficient workspace can help your organization deliver its service to customers at the right time and at the right price.

Several causes of waste are common in the service industry:

- unnecessary movement of people, paper, and information,
- delays that result in waiting,
- overproduction, with a service provided faster or in larger volumes than the customer requires,
- failure to deliver what the customer needs, and

- unnecessary processes or procedures that slow service delivery.

Many financial services – such as accounting, payroll management, and insurance claims processing – involve banking. The product of a transaction is the fulfillment of the customer's request, which could be a deposit of money, an insurance policy, or a bill payment. Often, this data is delivered internally with one department providing it to another within an organization.

Accounting

You can map the value stream required to complete an accounting transaction, including information retrieval, spreadsheet creation, data entry, and the delivery of the service.

Using this type of map, you can continually check for and eliminate any duplications or unnecessary steps, to eliminate waste.

Payroll

You can improve payroll management by making small, local, and continuous changes to processes, such as regular updates of banking details. It's a good idea to provide rewards for employees who generate cost- and time-saving processes.

Claims processing

You can optimize the work environment and processes in insurance companies' Claim departments by forming assembly lines for paperwork processing and by removing cubicles so that employees work in modular teams.

In healthcare, the aims of a Lean approach are to improve turnaround time, contain costs, reduce space requirements, increase the speed of delivery, and improve the quality of patient care.

It involves identifying and removing wasteful activities and focusing on those activities that add value for patients.

In the context of healthcare, a Lean approach focuses on eliminating waste in various ways:

- keeping laboratories close to testing sites,
- basing testing on patient needs and ensuring no unnecessary tests are performed,
- organizing workspaces so that nurses and patients don't have to travel distances to retrieve equipment or to be tested,
- minimizing inventory and queues, such as lab samples waiting to be processed and patients waiting for beds, and
- reducing the amount of paperwork needed to process patients and treatments.

Question

Given what you have learned about implementing Lean in the service industry, how do you think it could be applied in the retail industry?

Options:

1. Place the right product in its correct place at the right time using visual cues
2. Using point-of-sale information to stimulate supply and delivery based on purchases
3. Minimize inventory levels
4. Keep shop floors and back offices clean and ordered
5. Minimize interactions with customers by automating most processes

Answer:

Positive interactions with customers are value-added processes. Automating this is seldom useful in retail.

Another example of implementing Lean in retail is the first-in, first-out principle used for stocking retail shelves. The newest stock is placed at the back of the shelf so that older stock is purchased first. This principle is particularly useful for perishable stock.

Question

Match industry examples with how Lean principles are applied to them.

Options:

A. Manufacturing
B. Banking
C. Healthcare
D. Retail

Targets:

1. Produce product components only as they're needed
2. Remove unwanted activities in the processing of mortgage applications using value stream mapping
3. Place testing laboratories close to sample stations
4. Use a point-of-sale device to link to inventory

Answer:

In manufacturing, you need to work with the JIT principle of producing goods only as they are needed.

Value stream mapping helps banks identify and possibly remove wasteful activities in the processing of mortgage and loan applications.

In the healthcare industry, you can reduce wasteful movement by placing laboratories close to sample stations.

In the retail industry, you can directly link sales to inventory, using point-of-sale devices.

SECTION 2 - THE FIVE STEPS TO LEAN

SECTION 2 - The Five Steps to Lean

To implement Lean, you follow a five-step process. First you identify value, or what a customer is willing to pay for. Next you map the value stream, create current and future state maps, and develop an action plan. The third step is to create flow in the value stream by organizing people, ensuring quality at the source, and using reliable, well-maintained equipment.

Establishing pull is the fourth step. It optimizes flow by basing production on real-time consumption. Ways to do this include leveling production, using kanban, and optimizing supply and delivery. The fifth step is to seek perfection through continuous improvement. The PDCA cycle is a common methodology for implementing this.

INTRODUCTION OF THE FIVE STEPS

Introduction of the five steps

To reach your destination, you need a map. A five-step process can help you implement Lean and begin reaping its benefits. First you identify value and map the value stream. You create flow, establish pull, and, finally, seek perfection. The final step then leads back to the first step, creating a cycle.

Identify value

Identifying value involves finding out what your customers actually want and how much it's worth to them.

Map the value stream

Mapping the value stream involves outlining all processes, tasks, and information needed to develop a product or service and deliver it to your customers.

Create flow

To create flow, you remove interruptions, bottlenecks, and periods of inactivity from the value stream.

Establish pull

Establishing pull involves creating a system in which customer demand drives production. Products or services are created only once customers demand them. Similarly, goods and information are supplied or moved only when they're required.

Seek perfection

The last step, of seeking perfection, is a continuous process of finding ways to improve on the first four steps.

Question

Sequence the steps of the Lean process in order.

Options:

A. Identify value
B. Map the value stream
C. Create flow
D. Establish pull
E. Seek perfection

Answer:

Identify value is ranked the first step. The first step in implementing Lean is to identify value.

Map the value stream is ranked the second step. Once you've identified value, you map the value stream.

Create flow is ranked the third step. The third step in the Lean process is to create flow.

Establish pull is ranked the fourth step. Establishing pull is the fourth step in implementing Lean.

Seek perfection is ranked the fifth step. The fifth step in the Lean process is to seek perfection.

IDENTIFY AND MAP VALUE

Identify and map value

First you should define value for each product or service your organization offers. This gives direction to the entire organization's work processes, determining what, how, and whether it should provide specific goods or services. In Lean thinking, the customer defines value. The customer can be a person, team, or company using your product.

The value a customer assigns to a product depends on factors like the product's quality, capabilities, and price, and on how well it meets the customer's expectations. Customers of a casual clothing retailer, for instance, may place a high premium on variety, style, and affordability. Customers of a more upmarket retailer may assign greater value to quality and personal service.

The customers of a healthcare provider are likely to value rapid service, accuracy, professional expertise, empathetic treatment, and a tranquil environment. The heart of identifying value is to understand what your customers' key requirements are. You also need to stay in touch with changes in these requirements – so identifying value is an ongoing process.

Market research for a chain of clothing stores, for example, reveals that customers value the look of the stores, friendly service, clothing quality, and the garment alteration service that the stores provide. The result of the research is an accurate profile of the service and products customers really want the stores to provide.

Once you've identified value, you map your organization's value stream, including all the steps used to bring a product or service from conception to delivery to the customer. The goal in doing this is to help you identify and eliminate waste – any steps that don't produce value or create obstacles in its flow to the customer.

So how do you map a value stream? First you walk backward through the entire production process. Then you draw current and future state maps. Finally, you develop an action plan for moving from the current to the future state.

Walk backward through the process

Inspect a process from the time you delivered a product or service to the first step involved in creating or designing it. While doing this, consider how orders are processed, what triggers each subsequent stage in the process, and when products are checked for errors.

Draw maps

You need to draw up two value stream maps. The first – known as a current state map – records what is currently occurring, including information such as wait times, resources, tasks, and processes.

The second map outlines the ideal process, known as the future state of the value stream.

Lean for Business Organizations

Develop an action plan

Once you have the current and future state maps, you develop a practical action plan to fix the current errors and move toward the future state map. This plan should involve all employees, who must participate in continuously improving their work functions.

Question

As the manager of a well-established plastic toy manufacturer, you're currently implementing a Lean approach in an effort to reduce costs and add value.

How can you identify value and map the value stream for your company?

Options:

1. Establish what the toy retailers your company supplies really want and appreciate

2. Examine the process for creating and delivering each product, map the current process and an ideal process, and then plan appropriate changes

3. Review your company's quarterly financial reports

4. Boost marketing for a new range of educational toys your company has manufactured to generate more demand

Answer:

Option 1: This option is correct. In this example, toy retailers are your company's customers. Identifying value involves establishing what they value about the products or service your company provides.

Option 2: This is a correct option. Mapping the value stream means you walk backward through the process, draw up current and future state maps, and develop an action plan.

Option 3: This option is incorrect. In the context of a Lean approach, value refers to what customers value, rather than to financial values like those in quarterly or annual company reports.

Option 4: This option is incorrect. A Lean approach focuses on establishing "pull" – with production tailored based on existing customer demand, rather than with demand manipulated to suit production.

CREATE FLOW

Create flow

Once you've analyzed the value stream in your organization, the next step is to optimize the flow of value through it. This involves removing obstacles and bottlenecks. Three strategies for creating flow are organizing people, ensuring quality at the source, and ensuring that equipment is reliable and well maintained.

Employees should be organized into cross-functional teams comprised of people who can fulfil all the functions required to make a product or complete a service. These teams should take ownership of safety, product value, and waste reduction. Ensuring quality at the source means checking quality throughout production, rather than as a separate step at the end of production. You can ensure quality through source inspection, progressive inspection, and error-proofing.

Source inspection

With source inspection, employees check their work before passing it onto the next phase.

For example, at the end of a call in which a customer applies for a credit card, a call center representative checks to ensure he has recorded all the customer's personal information and this person's needs before passing on the paperwork to the next employee, who processes the application. This second employee must check the form to ensure all the required fields have been completed correctly.

Progressive inspection

Progressive inspection is the standardized inspection each employee carries out before beginning work on a component. This avoids investing time and effort on a faulty product, and reduces risk.

For instance, bank tellers inspect checks methodically before stamping and processing them.

Error-proofing

To reduce the need for inspection, you can provide built-in features that prevent errors from occurring. This is known as error-proofing – or referred to using the Japanese term poka-yoke.

For example, online retail sites have logic checks to ensure customers enter all required details before allowing them to progress to the next page.

All employees should share responsibility for performing maintenance tasks on a daily basis. For example, team members should routinely clean and maintain the equipment they use.

Question

As the operations manager in a toy factory, you want to improve flow in the production of jigsaw puzzles. The puzzles need to be designed, printed, glued, cut, and packaged.

What suggestions could you make to improve value stream flow in the toy factory?

Options:

1. Create a single team to produce the puzzles, from design right through to packing for delivery

2. Create a protocol for print operators to check whether puzzle designs are correctly laid out before printing them

3. Use specialized glue dispensers to prevent uneven application

4. Ensure operators keep the area around the cutting press clear and free of clutter

5. Create a specialized work team to focus exclusively on puzzle design

6. Use the largest available space to glue, cut, and package puzzles

Answer:

Option 1: This option is correct. You can improve flow by organizing people into cross-functional teams that take specific product groups through the entire production process.

Option 2: This option is correct. Progressively inspecting products before commencing work is an example of ensuring quality at source, which encourages good flow.

Option 3: This is a correct option. Removing the possibility of mistakes through error-proofing prevents waste and encourages good flow.

Option 4: This option is correct. Keeping work areas clean and neat helps prevent disruptions to flow, as well as improving safety.

Option 5: This option is incorrect. To improve flow, you should organize people into cross-functional teams with members that cooperate throughout a process.

Option 6: This option is incorrect. To create flow, work areas should be relatively compact so that components and tools can move quickly from one person to the next.

ESTABLISH PULL

Establish pull

Establishing pull is about supplying products at the same rate at which the consumer demands or consumes them. You let customer demand pull production, instead of pushing products out to the customer based on forecasts. The concept of pull builds on the basis of good flow in the value stream, and improves it further by reducing inventory and reducing the time it takes to produce a product – known as cycle time.

The aim is to communicate real-time requirements to trigger production at each step. This synchronizes production so products are made only as needed. To move your organization from a push to a pull system, you level out production, use kanban to signal replenishment, and adjust supply and delivery logistics.

Level out production

You can level out production by logically sequencing it rather than creating and storing batches of components. How you sequence production depends on available working hours, cycle time, and the number of products the customer requires.

Suppose you have an order for 5,000 digital cameras. With leveled out production, you create 5,000 camera components simultaneously. You time production so team members don't have to wait for components to complete their tasks.

Use kanban

Kanban is the signaling system used to trigger replenishment of inventory or the components needed to complete a task based on what's used at a particular station. Kanban signals may be as simple as an empty space or container. You can also use cards, e- mails, or flashing lights. For example, a light flashes just before a stamping machine completes a set, allowing the operator to prepare its next load.

Adjust supply and delivery logistics

Supply and delivery has to be fast and reliable to ensure flow, and this requires elegant logistics. For example, you might provide suppliers with delivery windows in which products must be delivered. On the other end, you could arrange product delivery so that you drop multiple products off to different customers during the same delivery run.

Question

Your toy factory has traditionally kept a large component inventory and created toys in batches. It orders and delivers single types of items in bulk.

How would you convert the company's current system from a push to a pull system?

Options:

1. Synchronize production so that while some workers are assembling components, others are manufacturing the components they need

2. Replace the large container next to the molding machine with two smaller trolleys. When one empties, it's refilled

3. Drop off multiple toy store orders in the same delivery run

4. Create demand through direct sales strategies

5. Only deliver toys once the delivery van is loaded to capacity

Answer:

Option 1: This option is correct. To establish pull, you should level out production so that toys flow evenly through the manufacturing process. This reduces inventory and cycle time.

Option 2: This option is correct. To establish pull, you use kanban to signal replenishment requests, reducing inventory and cycle time.

Option 3: This option is correct. Establishing pull requires efficient delivery logistics.

Option 4: This option is incorrect. Pushing products onto customers doesn't create pull.

Option 5: This option is incorrect. This is an example of muda – it would inhibit the continuous flow of products to the customer.

SEEK PERFECTION

Seek perfection

The final step in Lean implementation is to continuously seek perfection – identifying and incrementally modifying practices that can be improved. A useful tool in implementing continuous improvement is the Plan-Do-Check-Act cycle, known for short as PDCA.

Plan

During the plan stage of the PDCA cycle, managers and employees collaborate to identify problems or inefficiencies. Then they identify the causes of these problems and work out the steps needed to resolve them. Finally, the team predicts what the results of this change will be.

Do

In the Do phase, team leaders communicate the plan and assign goals to all stakeholders. Then a set of employees carries out procedures on a trial-run basis and makes preliminary changes.

Check

During the check phase, team leaders assess results to find out if the changes have been successful or whether further modifications are required.

Act

When improvements have been verified, they become the new standard operating procedure and may also be implemented on a broader scale.

A team in a clothing retail store establishes that customers often struggle to find items in the sizes they want. Follow along as the team works through the PDCA cycle.

Plan: The team members realize that the problem is occurring because the size labels on garments aren't immediately noticeable. They decide on using different colored hangers for each size to improve the customer's experience.

Do: Purchasers and retail assistants are told of the new plan and hangers in different colors are produced, distributed, and used.

Check: Next the team assesses the results. It notices that shoppers take a while to understand the color coding, so a code map is developed and placed on each rack.

Act: The change is a success, so the color system is standardized and rolled out to all stores in the franchise.

Question

The toy factory's value stream is flowing well and pull has been established.

What should you do next?

Options:

1. Encourage teams to keep identifying problems and their causes, and to develop plans to address them

2. Modify processes to address production problems, assess how successful the modifications are, and standardize successful procedures

3. Identify changing values by researching toy retailer trends

4. Walk backwards through the production process, from the delivery of finished products to the design of the toys

Answer:

Option 1: This option is correct. The first step in seeking perfection is to plan collaboratively to identify and rectify problems and inefficiencies. The plan should include desired outcomes.

Option 2: This is a correct option. After planning around improvements, you carry out the changes on a preliminary basis, then check and tweak processes, and finally you act by establishing new work protocols.

Option 3: This option is incorrect. You need to pursue perfection by implementing the PDCA cycle. If this cycle identifies changes in customer value as a problem, you can then implement this step.

Option 4: This option is incorrect. After planning to solve problems, you implement solutions and check their efficacy, before creating new standard procedures.

SECTION 3 - INTEGRATING LEAN AND SIX SIGMA

SECTION 3 - Integrating Lean and Six Sigma

Lean and Six Sigma are complementary production management methodologies with many important similarities. Although their focus, tools, and results time frames differ, they create a powerful hybrid when used in combination.

The unique business conditions that your organization faces will affect the methodology and tools you choose. When making these decisions, you need to consider time frames, financial commitment, the nature and pervasiveness of the problems your organization is facing, and your organization's ability to adopt a culture change.

When implementing Lean and Six Sigma, it's often simplest to start with short-term Lean improvement projects. These provide fast results and usually reveal deeper and more pervasive problems. Then you implement Six Sigma, with its robust tools and methods, to address problems.

COMPARING LEAN AND SIX SIGMA

Comparing Lean and Six Sigma

Lean is one of many improvement methodologies in use today focused on reducing wastes, creating value, and streamlining operations. This topic shows how Lean relates to one of the most popular of these improvement methodologies – Six Sigma.

Six Sigma is an organization-wide improvement initiative that aims to reduce variation and defects in processes to achieve near perfection in goods and services.

It minimizes defects and improves processes to deliver products and services that meet customer requirements, using statistical and other tools.

Six Sigma relies on a five-step process improvement methodology – DMAIC – which stands for Define, Measure, Analyze, Improve, and Control. This tool helps organizations understand and minimize process variation.

Define

The first step in the DMAIC process is to define the problem, the project goals, and the customer deliverables.

Measure

As the second step, you measure the process inputs and outputs to determine current performance. This quantifies the problem defined in the first step.

Analyze

The third step is to analyze the data generated in the first two steps to determine the root cause or causes of the defects.

Improve

After analysis, you improve the process by eliminating defects or variations.

Control

The final step integrates the concept of continuous improvement. In this step, you control the improved process by monitoring future process performance.

While Lean and Six Sigma evolved from different paths, the two methodologies have several things in common:
- both are inspired by the plan, do, check, act cycle known as PDCA,
- both use systematic problem-solving tools,
- both depend on project teams and supporting specialists,
- both require employee participation that often results in widespread behavioral and system changes, and
- both deliver significant bottom-line benefits.

However, there are some significant differences between the two approaches. These include differences in methodology focus, customer focus, results timescale, tools, and training and awareness. Lean's focus on increasing speed results in decreases in lead time – the time between initiation and completion of a process.

Six Sigma's focus on reducing errors aims to reduce defects so that products or services are 99.9997% error free. Although Lean provides fast results, your organization's efforts must persist over the long term if you're to realize continued improvements. With Six Sigma, mid-term and long-term results are the main focus.

Question

Match characteristics to either the Lean or Six Sigma methodologies.

Options:

A. Aims to eliminate needless costs and effort
B. Focuses on creating value
C. Focuses on analyzing information visually and holistically
D. Aims to standardize products
E. Aims to prevent defects in goods and services
F. Focuses on using statistics to analyze information

Targets:

1. Lean
2. Six Sigma

Answer

Lean focuses on eliminating needless costs and effort – or waste, on providing goods and services that customers find valuable, and on using holistic, visual analyses.

Six Sigma aims to dramatically reduce or eliminate defects and variation, and focuses on the use of statistical tools to analyze information.

BUSINESS CONDITIONS

Business conditions

A government's Finance Department began implementing Six Sigma five years ago. This has resulted in a dramatic decrease in errors. However, the department remains unwieldy, slow, and costly to run. To eliminate waste and to speed up processes, the department realizes it needs to incorporate Lean thinking into its system.

Darren is a senior manager in the Tax Division of the Finance Department. Follow along as he considers how Lean could be used to create the optimal system.

The Tax Division is working accurately and running a tight ship. Our macro- policies and logistical processes are sound. They generate good information and revenue has gone up, so our service is of good quality.

But taxpayers complain that they have to fill in too many long and difficult forms, so compliance is costly and time-consuming for them. Lean can help us focus on meeting their expectations.

Processing the forms wastes a lot of time on our side too. On the whole, our operating costs are much too high. So Lean could help us save time and moneyby cutting out waste.

Adopting Lean could be quick – we could use it to optimize our forms almost immediately and then go on to find other problems that might be relatively quick to fix.

Although relatively inexpensive, Lean requires a serious commitment because it's not just a tool – it's an ongoing philosophy that everyone has to adopt.

Although Lean and Six Sigma originated as two different strategies, they're increasingly being viewed as complementary processes. By creating a Lean Six Sigma hybrid, Darren can combine the strengths of both methodologies and gain access to a larger range of tools for production management.

You need to decide what tools to apply in different improvement initiatives. You can base these decisions on various criteria – the required time frame and financial commitment, the nature of the primary problem, the organization's ability to adopt a culture change, and the pervasiveness of the problem.

Answering questions related to each factor can help you choose which elements of which methodology – Lean or Six Sigma – will apply to your organization.

Time frame and financial commitment

Do you need a quick, relatively inexpensive strategy for reducing cycle time? Or is it feasible and worthwhile to apply rigorous statistical analysis to uncover the roots of the problem? Lean provides fast results and is less expensive than Six Sigma, which requires longer time frames and complex data analysis.

Nature of primary problem

What is the primary problem that you need to address? Is it waste and speed? Or is it defects and variation in processes? Lean reduces waste and increases speed. Six Sigma addresses defects and variation in processes.

Ability to adopt culture change

Does your organization's corporate culture support change?

Both Lean and Six Sigma are better implemented in an organization that supports change. However, the longer time frame available for implementing Six Sigma allows change to take place even if the organization's culture is not very supportive of change. On the other hand, due to a relatively short time frame, Lean may not be the best approach if your organization's culture means that people are likely to resist new ways of thinking and new ways of doing things.

Pervasiveness of problem

How pervasive is the problem? Is it isolated and relatively simple to fix? Or does it permeate the entire process? Lean is useful for problems that are relatively simple to fix. Six Sigma is best for addressing more pervasive problems related to production.

Question

Match each description of a business condition to the methodology that best addresses it. More than one condition may match a single methodology.

Options:

A. "Given our financial picture, we need to achieve many small improvements without high cost."

B. "The new manufacturing processes are taking too long. We have to reduce the time they take, and this has to happen soon!"

C. "After the drop in quality in last year's new models, our customer base is deserting us in droves. We've got to get our base back!"

D. "We're accepting way too much variation to remain competitive for long. The problem seems to be throughout the organization."

Targets:

1. Lean
2. Six Sigma

Answer:

Lean can be implemented and yield results quickly and is less expensive than Six Sigma. It's ideal for addressing isolating problems and inefficiencies, and can be implemented while people are still getting used to a new way of thinking.

Six Sigma's focus is on improving quality by reducing variation and eliminating product defects. It's useful for addressing pervasive problems, but takes longer and is more expensive to implement than Lean.

NEEDS-BASED INTEGRATION

Needs-based integration

Combining Lean and Six Sigma enables you to improve quality, achieve maximum process speed, and reduce costs and waste. However, every organization is unique and requires its own mix of Lean and Six Sigma tools.

You may choose to apply a combination of the statistical tools that Six Sigma offers so that you have metrics to gauge success toward achieving your goals. In addition, using the more holistic tools that Lean offers can help employees understand the role they play in overall improvement.

Despite the benefits of a Lean-Six Sigma hybrid, adopting both methodologies in parallel can cause confusion. It's often simplest to start with short-term Lean improvement projects, which provide fast results and usually reveal deeper and more pervasive problems. Then you can implement Six Sigma, with its robust tools and methods, to address these problems.

Starting with Lean has a number of advantages. With Lean, an organization can quickly standardize its basic flow, eliminate steps that don't add value, and reduce inventory. The quick results and cost savings Lean provides help prove the benefits of a process improvement initiative and so encourage support for it. A multinational healthcare services provider initiated a push to become the industry leader. To do this, it implemented Lean and Six Sigma.

Lean

The company initiated more than 100 small improvement projects, with the objective of improving the supply chain by removing waste and steps that don't add value. Within a year, this objective was met, with a cost savings of $250 million, improved quality, and greater customer satisfaction.

Six Sigma

After implementing Lean principles, the company adopted Six Sigma to maintain the improvements and to address defects that the initial improvement efforts revealed. During the first three years of Six Sigma implementation, the company realized over $500 million in savings. It deployed Black Belts and Green Belts across the organization to ensure continual improvement.

Combining Lean and Six Sigma can have benefits for organizations in a range of businesses. Some examples include manufacturing, market research, and financial sector businesses.

Manufacturing

A playground equipment manufacturer cut lead time by 92%, improved productivity by more than 20%, and reduced scrap from 0.8% to 0.2% by implementing Lean.

However, a defect in the manufacturing processes was creating holes in the PVC-coated pipes, causing a high volume of scrap. Lean tools couldn't identify the cause of the defects. By implementing Six Sigma, the company accessed the tools and approach needed to identify the cause of the problem, analyze it, improve the situation, and control the improvements.

Marketing research

The owner of a marketing research company wants to improve operations by employing a quick, relatively inexpensive strategy to reduce process waste and lead times. The owner's best strategy is to implement Lean, which produces the quick fixes he requires. He applies 5S to improve individual work speeds and installs software that speeds up information processing and the analysis of results. If serious quality issues with regard to analysis and research reports are found through the process, the owner may need to think about a longer-term strategy, such as implementing Six Sigma as well.

Financial

The executive board of a multi-national financial organization is committing a large amount of time and money toward continuous process improvement. The board wants to eliminate waste – such as unnecessary duplication and time wasted during meetings. It also wants to increase speed in the organization's operations and to eliminate variation in processes. For this organization, a combination of Lean and Six Sigma tools and methods is appropriate. Lean will eliminate waste and increase process speed. Six Sigma will address variation in the company's processes. For example, using a standardized form and database reduces accounting errors.

Question

A multinational retail chain is struggling to retain its market share due to increased competition. The executive board establishes process improvement goals. The company needs to become faster and more responsive to customers, achieve near-perfect quality service, streamline processes, and use statistics to monitor improvements. The board wants to realize immediate results but is also willing to make a long-term financial commitment.

Which approach is best?

Options:

1. Implement Six Sigma to enable quick improvements to produce near-perfect quality service and to access its large toolkit for monitoring improvements

2. Implement Lean to enable the company to become faster and more responsive and achieve near- perfect quality

3. Adopt Lean to streamline processes and obtain immediate results, and then implement Six Sigma to improve customer satisfaction and monitor processes

4. Implement Lean and Six Sigma simultaneously – use Lean to address immediate problems while setting up DMAIC to begin long-term improvement efforts

Answer:

Option 1: This option is incorrect. Six Sigma will help the company meet its goals of near-perfect quality and statistical monitoring, but it may not help it become faster or streamline its processes.

Option 2: This option is incorrect. Lean will help the company to streamline its service and become more responsive. However, Lean doesn't focus on achieving near-perfect quality or provide a range of statistical tools for monitoring performance.

Option 3: This is the correct option. This retailer requires a two-pronged approach – implement Lean first to address waste in basic processes, and then implement Six Sigma for longer-term improvement and statistical monitoring.

Option 4: This is an incorrect option. Adopting the methodologies simultaneously may result in confusion. It's generally easiest to implement Lean first and then to implement Six Sigma.

CHAPTER II - USING LEAN FOR PERFECTION AND QUALITY

CHAPTER II - Using Lean for Perfection and Quality
   SECTION 1 - 5S: Workplace Organization and Standardization
   SECTION 2 - Fundamentals of Lean: Hoshin Kanri
   SECTION 3 - Fundamentals of Lean: Jidoka and Poka Yoke

SECTION 1 - 5S: WORKPLACE ORGANIZATION AND STANDARDIZATION

SECTION 1 - 5S: Workplace Organization and Standardization

To improve efficiency and safety, and to reduce work-related stress, you can implement Lean's 5S methodology to ensure clean and well-ordered work areas. The steps in 5S include sort, set in order, shine, standardize, and sustain. First items should be sorted and any unnecessary items should be removed.

The remaining items and equipment should then be placed to promote sequential work flow and ease of movement. It's also important to use visual cues to help employees find items or to issue relevant safety warnings. Work areas and equipment should be cleaned and maintained, and then processes and routines should be standardized. Finally, the 5S practices should be sustained through monitoring and support.

WHY KEEP THINGS NEAT?

Why keep things neat?

Have you ever had to work in a messy environment? If you have, you'll know how frustrating and awkward it can be. Simply finding things takes time and it's difficult to get anything done. In contrast, a neat and uncluttered workspace gives you a sense of clarity and control. Everything is in the right place, so you can work efficiently.

Ensuring your workspace is in order has several benefits:
- tools and materials are easy to find and use,
- your environment is pleasant to work in,
- you're less likely to make mistakes, and
- you're much more productive because you don't have to waste time and effort searching for things.

A costing clerk works in a messy office. Papers and files are stacked on his desk. Half his pens don't work and his drawers are stuffed with often unnecessary stationery.

As a result, it takes the clerk time to find anything – from a working pen or a stapler to an important document. He also struggles to concentrate, so it's likely he'll make mistakes.

The clerk decides to tidy and organize his office. He creates a color-coded filing system and positions it within arm's reach. He also throws out pens that don't work and tidies his stationery drawer so that everything he needs is at his fingertips.

Keeping things neat and organized gives him more space to work in and cuts out a lot of wasted time and effort.

Question

What are the benefits of keeping your workspace neat and clean?

Options:

1. You'll save time
2. You'll be able to access what you need to get things done efficiently
3. You'll be more productive
4. You'll be less stressed
5. You're less likely to suffer from repetitive stress injury
6. You'll be more creative

Answer:

Option 1: This option is correct. When your workspace is neat and clean, you don't waste time fiddling with things you don't need or trying to find the things you do.

Option 2: This option is correct. You know where to find things in an organized workspace, whenever you need them.

Option 3: This option is correct. A neat, clean workspace saves time and effort, so it boosts productivity.

Option 4: This option is correct. It's less stressful because it's easier to function if surfaces aren't cluttered and you know where everything is. It's also less stressful because an organized space is a more pleasant environment to work in than one that's untidy.

Option 5: This option is incorrect. An organized workspace reduces the likelihood of injury. However, it won't necessarily prevent repetitive strain injuries.

Option 6: This option is incorrect. Although you can think more clearly in a neat, organized environment, you won't necessarily be more creative.

IMPLEMENTING 5S

Implementing 5S

With Lean, you can achieve an orderly, tidy workspace by following the five-step process called 5S. In the original Japanese, these five steps were referred to as Sieri, Seiton, Sieso, Seiketsu, and Shitsuke. These terms can be translated as sort, set in order, shine, standardize, and sustain.

1. Sort

The first step is to sort through all the tools and materials in your workspace and mark any items that you don't really need with red tags. Red-tagged items should then be moved to a holding area and documented so that all discarded items are accounted for. Excess inventory, superfluous equipment, and duplicate items should be stored or moved to another workstation. Defective, obsolete, or useless items should be discarded. Before and after photographs are a quick and useful way of documenting the process.

2. Set in order

The second step is to place the tools and materials you need so that they're easy to find, use, and put away again. Everything should have a designated place that requires the least effort and motion to reach and use. Typically, you should place tools and equipment into a sequential arrangement according to the order in which you need them to complete your work. Creating visual cues such as paint marks, color-coding, and labels can help you to find and replace each item in its designated area.

3. Shine

Shine is about keeping things clean. Equipment and surfaces should be cleaned at least once a day, the floor should be swept, and designated areas should be re-painted regularly so they remain easy to identify. The shine step should be an integral and scheduled aspect of the daily work of all employees. For example, employees in a manufacturing plant should return tools to their places and wipe down surfaces they've used at the end of each shift. Inspection checklists and cleaning or painting schedules can help ensure this occurs.

4. Standardize

Processes for sorting, setting in order, and shining workspaces should be standardized so that everyone knows their responsibilities, the steps can be performed quickly and efficiently, and performing them becomes a habit. For example, the process for opening a new customer file may be standardized to include labeling the file, placing the file in the correct drawer, and adding the customer's contact details to a customer database. These standards should be clearly displayed. Anyone who opens a new customer file will then follow these steps and quickly become competent in doing so.

5. Sustain

Once processes for keeping work environments clean and orderly have been set up, it's important to sustain them. Employees have to be regularly monitored and evaluated to ensure compliance. They also need to buy in to the process. So everyone needs to understand why 5S is important, have enough time to implement the steps, and receive the required support from their managers and team leaders. Offering rewards or recognition is useful, as is including designated clean-up times in work schedules.

When you sort work environments to remove unwanted items, you need to involve the right people. Management has to support the process, but the people who should do the actual sorting are the employees on the ground. Everyone on a team should work together to sort the space the team uses.

In a team context, you can follow these steps to coordinate the sorting process:
1. designate an area for unwanted items,
2. establish criteria for deciding if an item is needed,
3. identify and tag unnecessary items,
4. put red-tagged items into the designated area, and
5. 5. give team leaders or managers the responsibility of dealing with the unwanted items – disposing, donating, reallocating, or returning the items to the workspace.

Visual information is a key concept in Lean manufacturing. At the moment when you need something, you should be able to locate it at a glance. Information is provided at the point of need.

You can use visual cues when applying 5S in a variety of ways:

- using labels or drawing lines to indicate where things belong,
- displaying specifications and measurements directly on equipment or work surfaces,
- signposting hazardous equipment, materials, or processes with eye-catching displays, such as warning lights or symbols,
- streamlining inventory with kanban cards,
- providing feedback on machine performance by displaying gauges and guidelines in the operator's line of sight,
- arranging workspaces so people can communicate easily with their colleagues, and
- displaying performance measures and procedural guidelines where employees can refer to them.

Suppose a line supervisor is implementing 5S in the sewing division of a garment manufacturing company. The supervisor has already led employees in sorting the area by removing all unnecessary items and now wants to implement the next four steps.

2. Set in order

The supervisor assists the employees in arranging their workstations and the items they use to maximize comfort and efficiency. For instance, right-handed employees ensure their scissors are hooked within reach of their right hands, with pieces awaiting work kept on the left of their sewing machines. They can then pick up fabric and sew or cut threads without fumbling or hesitating.

Pieces awaiting processing are stacked on a common set of shelves, with marked and labeled spaces. The employee who prepares the fabric upstream stacks them whenever the designated spaces on the shelf are emptied.

3. Shine

Employees sweep their sewing surface and machine clear of debris after working on each piece. At the end of each day, tools are hung up, the area is tidied, the floor is swept, and everything is wiped down. A schedule is also set for oiling sewing machine parts on a weekly basis.

4. Standardize

Time is set aside at the end of each day for cleaning and tidying. The supervisor explains why 5S is important so that the garment workers buy into the concept. In consultation with employees, the supervisor also sets out protocols for regular sorting, setting in order, and shining of workstations.

5. Sustain

Posters are put on the wall to educate workers about 5S. Cleanliness is rewarded with a monthly prize. The supervisor regularly checks up on workstations and areas, and offers assistance by ensuring employees have the right fixtures and equipment in place. For example, they should each have labeled shelving, brushes for cleaning, and a small box of spare spools.

Implementing 5S creates a pleasant, orderly environment for the garment workers. It improves the accuracy and speed of their workmanship, and allows for better flow in the production cycle.

Now review how 5S can be implemented in a service environment. Follow along as the first two steps of the process are conducted at a call center.

The supervisor explains the benefits of 5S and why it should be applied. Then each team member red-tags items they don't use at their stations. Red-tagged items are placed in the photocopy room, where the supervisor sorts through them.

Electronic information that's not used is flagged and IT personnel are brought in to delete or move this information.

The team members place colored tags on sections of the complaint-handling manual to help them find information they need often more quickly.

Service consultants keep jotting paper on the right of their computers so there's no need to twist or move away from the keyboard when writing notes.

A working pen is kept directly above the paper. This layout is swapped for left-handed consultants.

On their computers, team members create desktop shortcuts to the information and forms they use most often.

In addition, trays for ongoing issues, courtesy call backs, and resolved issues are color coded and placed on shelves within easy reach of each of the consultants.

To implement the shine step at the call center, employees dust and clean telephone and computer equipment. They tidy their workstations and place all notes in the correct trays. They also run system cleanup programs on their computers. To standardize 5S, call center operators are issued with checklists of 5S chores. For example, they're expected to place all notes in the correct trays and to update the company database at the end of each call.

At the end of each shift, team members are expected to tidy their work areas and to delete unnecessary e-mails. A schedule for computer maintenance tasks is also set up. To sustain 5S, the supervisor regularly monitors the team and rewards compliant operators. The newly-formed standards are displayed in locations where they're accessible to everyone throughout the call center. Also, a 15-minute cleanup period is scheduled for the end of each shift.

SECTION 2 - FUNDAMENTALS OF LEAN: HOSHIN KANRI

SECTION 2 - Fundamentals of Lean: Hoshin Kanri

Hoshin Kanri is a methodology for managing strategic direction. It's a continuous improvement strategy that aligns with the PDCA cycle. The planning phase of a Hoshin Kanri initiative maps to the plan step in PDCA. At this point, you develop strategic objectives to address current problems and an action plan to meet these objectives.

The execution phase maps to the do and check steps of PDCA. Here you implement the action plan and monitor its success using the agreed metrics. The reflection phase maps to the act step of PDCA. You determine the success of the project. If the objectives have been met, you standardize the planned tactics. If the objectives haven't been met, you identify corrective actions and move through the cycle again.

HOSHIN KANRI AND PDCA

Hoshin Kanri and PDCA

A philosophy surrounding the ancient art of Japanese sword fighting emphasizes the concept of "ho" – meaning strategy or method. The belief is that the more familiar you are with strategy, the more likely you are to identify your enemy's intentions – and so to win. In business, a similar focus on strategy is found in the approach called Hoshin Kanri.

The word Hoshin comprises two Japanese characters – "ho," meaning strategy or method, and "shin," meaning compass or needle. Together the words mean a method or way for setting strategic direction.

The word Kanri is also comprised of two characters – "kan," meaning control, and "ri," meaning reason. Together these words can be interpreted as management. So placing all these meanings together, Hoshin Kanri is a methodology for setting and managing strategic direction.

The Hoshin Kanri methodology is designed to help businesses adjust fast, be innovative, and align their actions and innovations with clear strategic goals. Using

Hoshin Kanri, you envision an ideal future for your business and then develop strategies that help to make that vision a reality.

Question

Identify the correct translations of the terms "hoshin" and "kanri."

Options:

1. Hoshin means setting a strategic direction
2. Kanri means using logic and control, or management
3. Hoshin means strategic management
4. Kanri means directional control

Answer:

Option 1: This option is correct. "Ho" means method and "shin" means compass. Together they mean setting a strategic direction.

Option 2: This is a correct option. "Kan" means control and "ri" means logic or reason. Together they can be interpreted to mean management.

Option 3: This option is incorrect. Although "shin" means compass, "ho" means method. Together they mean setting a strategic direction.

Option 4: This is an incorrect option. Although "kan" means control, "ri" means reason or logic. Together they can be interpreted to mean management.

Hoshin Kanri maps to the Plan-Do-Check-Act – or PDCA – cycle. Like the PDCA cycle, it's a dynamic approach that focuses on continuous improvement.

Plan

In the Plan phase, you assess and define the problem your organization faces. You determine its root cause by

asking why it's happening and you develop a strategy for dealing with it.
Do
In the Do phase, you implement the strategy you identified during planning.
Check
In the Check phase, you monitor the results of putting the plan in action to determine whether your strategy is working.
Act
In the Act phase, you standardize the strategy you implemented if it proved successful. If the strategy didn't succeed, you identify corrective actions for improving it. This takes you back to the start of the cycle, where you plan to address the problem.

The Act phase links to the Plan phase in a cycle of continuous improvement. You assess the results of putting a plan into action. Then you repeat the steps of planning, implementing, monitoring, and assessing results to continue improving your operations.

Question
Match each step in the PDCA cycle to a corresponding action.
Options:
A. Plan
B. Do
C. Check
D. Act
Targets:
1. Define the problem
2. Implement the strategy
3. Monitor the results

4. Standardize or correct strategies to ensure the desired results

Answer:

In the plan phase, you define the problem and develop a strategy to address it.

In the do phase, you implement the strategy identified during planning.

In the check phase, you monitor the results of the strategy implemented in the do phase.

In the act phase, you standardize the strategy if it succeeded or revise the strategy so it will have the desired results.

PLANNING

Planning

A plastics manufacturer is losing market share to its competition. Executive managers propose using a Hoshin Kanri initiative to find out why customers are leaving the business and to address the problem. The initiative is divided into three stages – planning, execution, and reflection.

The planning stage of the Hoshin Kanri initiative maps to the plan phase of the PDCA cycle. During this phase, the team identifies increasing market share as an important objective. But to do this, it first needs to determine why the company's market share has dropped.

The team discovers that production costs are too high and on-time shipments of products are poor. Also, some competitors are promoting their use of biodegradable plastics in their products – and your company hasn't developed this type of plastic.

The team then develops a project plan, outlining its goals, metrics for monitoring progress, team members' responsibilities, and tactics for achieving the goals.

Goals

The project goals the team develops must align with the organization's strategic goals, and executive management must support them.

For the plastics company, the team sets the goals of its Hoshin Kanri initiative as reducing operating costs to 5% below those of the company's closest competitor, improving on-time shipment by 10%, and increasing product innovations by one new item per quarter.

Metrics

Metrics are standard measurements. In a Hoshin Kanri project, they enable you to measure actual performance and compare it to planned or desired performance. This information enables you to determine how well you're meeting the established goals.

Members of the team at the plastics company define various metrics for measuring progress in achieving the agreed goals. They determine that annual sales are at $25 million and aim to reach $28 million this year. Operational costs are at $15 million per year and they want to reduce this to $13 million. On-time shipment is currently at 65% and they aim to improve this to 75%. Finally, product innovations currently average five per quarter and they want to increase this to six per quarter.

The "team members" section of the project plan should list the names of the team members who will carry out the plan and the specific responsibilities of each team member. For example, four individuals are assigned the goal of reducing operational costs.

The "tactics" section describes the activities and sub-projects you'll use to achieve your goals. There are several things you can do to ensure tactics remain effective:

- directly align the tactics with your project goals,
- align them with the metrics you've developed,
- don't waste effort – include only the tactics you need to meet the goals, and
- clearly assign accountability to an individual who checks implementation.

The team's tactics for reducing operational costs include applying 5S practices around the injection-molding equipment for more ergonomic production.

To meet the goal of on-time shipments, the team maps best-route deliveries from different suppliers for on-time shipment. Similarly, installing diameter sensors will reduce product defects that require reworking, and so reduce lead times.

Streamlining design documentation and testing will speed up product innovation.

Question

A banking call center is receiving unacceptably high numbers of complaints about its service. The management team decides to implement a Hoshin Kanri initiative to address and correct the problems.

What should the team do as part of the planning phase for the initiative?

Options:

1. Classify complaints to search for their underlying causes

2. Set objectives such as improving the relationship with the bank's IT supplier, improving server up times, and streamlining the processes for handling complaints

3. Resolve to change server accessibility from 95% to 99% and reduce complaint-handling times from 7 minutes to 4 minutes

4. Identify tactics for achieving agreed objectives and assign responsibilities to specific team members

5. Train call center representatives in conflict resolution practices

6. Research IT suppliers and appoint a new supplier to ensure better server accessibility

Answer:

Option 1: This option is correct. The first step in Hoshin Kanri is planning, which involves identifying the problems and the root causes that require addressing.

Option 2: This option is correct. The planning step in Hoshin Kanri involves setting strategic objectives to address underlying problems.

Option 3: This is a correct option. The planning step in Hoshin Kanri includes establishing metrics that show current baselines and measure change objectives.

Option 4: This is a correct option. Tactics and strategies for achieving specific action plan tasks should be described and responsibilities assigned to team members.

Option 5: This option is incorrect. Training representatives would be part of the execution phase rather than the planning phase.

Option 6: This is an incorrect option. These actions would be part of the execution phase rather than the planning phase.

EXECUTION

Execution

The project execution stage in a Hoshin Kanri initiative aligns with the do and check steps in the PDCA cycle. During this stage, employees implement the tactics identified in the plan phase. They also monitor performance using the planned metrics. To ensure the agreed strategies are executed successfully, you should conduct weekly reviews of each sub-project, reiterating the goals set out in the plan.

During reviews, meet face-to-face with team members who are accountable for each project to assess progress and to determine the next steps to take. Always stick to the targets set during planning. Don't shift the goal posts to accommodate flaws in the plan. If a plan doesn't work, scrap it rather than changing it piecemeal.

During the execution phase of the plastics manufacturing company's Hoshin Kanri initiative, employees carry out the tactics outlined in the plan and the results are monitored weekly. For example, the team analyzes reports on costs and revenues which the accounting system generated and measure these against the target metrics.

It also checks process cycle times, on-time delivery statistics, and new product design development rates.

Question

Remember the banking call center? The team there made plans to improve server accessibility rates and its relationship with its IT supplier. It also planned to streamline the call center's processes for handling complaints.

Which activities should the team perform during the execution phase of its initiative?

Options:

1. Hold weekly meetings with the IT supplier to iron out issues and improve their working relationship

2. Train supervisors in new complaint-handling process

3. Monitor server accessibility levels and the time it takes to resolve complaints using the new processes

4. Rework the plan so that server maintenance tasks and metrics are included

5. Reset complaint-handling time targets so they're easier to reach

Answer:

Option 1: This option is correct. In the execution phase, tactics – such as holding regular meetings with suppliers – are implemented.

Option 2: This is a correct option. In the execution phase, the planned tactics – such as training employees in new processes – are implemented.

Option 3: This option is correct. In the execution phase, metrics – such as server accessibility and process cycle times – should be monitored.

Option 4: This is an incorrect option. Amending the plan isn't an execution activity. The plan should be finalized, with those sections included, before the team enters the execution phase of the initiative.

Option 5: This option is incorrect. The team should always stick to the targets set during planning unless they're subsequently found to be completely unrealistic.

REFLECTION

Reflection

The reflection stage of a Hoshin Kanri initiative aligns with the act step in the PDCA cycle. Many organizations fail to carry out this step effectively. To ensure it occurs, you need to incorporate reflection time into the schedule for the initiative. Perhaps offer incentives for identifying flaws in the process to discourage glossing over of problems.

As you reflect on the project, you standardize successful tactics so they're integrated into daily work practices and continue to be used. During the reflection phase, the plastics manufacturing team realizes that new processes and documentation procedures weren't maintained after they were initiated. To correct this, the team considers why this happened.

It realizes that the new processes weren't communicated well and were taught only once – so behavior didn't really change. The team decides to post checklists in the work area and to monitor employee compliance more closely, correcting workers on the spot as necessary until they use the proper procedures.

The plan is then updated with the tactic for monitoring compliance, and a person is assigned responsibility for it. This subproject then moves through the cycle, with the team finally reflecting on its success and, if necessary, returning again to planning.

Question

The banking call center has test run its project to improve IT service, server accessibility, and complaints handling processes. What should it do as part of the reflection phase?

Options:

1. Standardize weekly supplier meetings because this tactic reached its objectives

2. The objectives for the complaints-handling process weren't met, so the process should be reworked to provide agents with flexible resolution strategies

3. Identify root causes of customer complaints

4. Run regular maintenance on servers so that call center agents won't experience technical delays while inputting customer data

Answer:

Option 1: This option is correct. In the reflection phase, the center should standardize successful tactics, so they're integrated into daily work practices.

Option 2: This is a correct option. If tactics aren't successful, the center needs to consider corrective actions to improve the plan so that it provides the desired results.

Option 3: This option is incorrect. During the reflection phase, the center assesses the success of the plan, standardizes successes, and considers corrective actions in areas that didn't meet targets. Identifying root causes of problems is part of the plan phase.

Option 4: This option is incorrect. Running maintenance on servers would be part of the execution phase.

SECTION 3 - FUNDAMENTALS OF LEAN: JIDOKA AND POKA YOKE

SECTION 3 - Fundamentals of Lean: Jidoka and Poka Yoke

Jidoka is a process that ensures problems are dealt with as they arise. It includes four steps – detect an abnormality or problem, stop the work process, fix the immediate problem, and finally install poka yoke to address the problem's root cause and prevent the problem from recurring.

INTRODUCING JIDOKA

Introducing jidoka

When you spot a problem or defect in something you're working on, should you finish your task and then try to deal with the problem? Should you throw away the defective item and carry on working on others? Or should you try to fix the problem before continuing work?

If you're following Lean principles, the production line stops as soon as defects occur. You then take steps to prevent the problem from occurring again – using an automated mechanism, if possible. This strategy is called jidoka.

The word jidoka is translated into English as "autonomation," which means intelligent automation or automation with a human touch. The concept was developed by Sakichi Toyota in 1902 as part of the Toyota Production System.

He noticed that broken threads were causing a mechanically powered loom to produce defective weaves. So he modified the loom to switch off automatically whenever it detected a broken thread. Jidoka became a central strategy in the Toyota Production System and has since become an integral part of the Lean approach.

Jidoka involves people or machines recognizing errors, providing feedback, and implementing countermeasures to rectify the errors immediately. This prevents defects from passing through to subsequent processes.

Jidoka also involves implementing measures to prevent errors from recurring. Where possible, these processes are automated using what's known as poka yoke. A poka yoke is any mechanism that automatically detects, prevents, or corrects errors.

Question

What benefits do you think jidoka can have?

Options:

1. Improved efficiency and productivity
2. Lower cost of production
3. Reduced need to repair or replace equipment
4. Near elimination of labor costs, with automated processes replacing employees
5. Higher quality output, with fewer defects in products
6. Removal of the need for employees to check quality

Answer:

Option 1: This option is correct. The use of automation with jidoka reduces the need for people to spend time repetitively correcting machine errors or reworking defective items. It also enables workers to staff multiple operations, stepping in only when automated processes have to be adjusted or modified. This results in greater efficiency and productivity.

Option 2: This is a correct option. Jidoka involves automating the detection and prevention of errors. This reduces defects and the time required to rework items, as well as boosting productivity. These benefits translate into lower overall costs of production and higher profitability.

Option 3: This option is correct. Because jidoka ensures problems are identified as they arise, poor performance or failures in equipment are dealt with promptly, forestalling problems before they can escalate.

Option 4: This option is incorrect. Although jidoka can enable you to deploy employees more effectively, it doesn't involve completely replacing employees with automated production systems.

Option 5: This is a correct option. A system that uses jidoka automatically detects and either prevents or corrects errors, resulting in higher quality output with fewer defects.

Option 6: This option is incorrect. In a jidoka system, both employees and automated mechanisms play important roles in detecting and preventing errors.

Implementing jidoka boosts productivity, reduces costs, helps prevent equipment failures, and results in higher product quality. But how can you apply jidoka in your work environment?

Implementing jidoka involves a four-step process. Either a person or a poka yoke detects a problem and then stops the work process. Someone is tasked to fix the immediate problem. And finally, you investigate the root cause of the problem and install a poka yoke or other measures to prevent it from occurring again.

DETECTING A PROBLEM

Detecting a problem

People can detect problems in three ways. The first is through observation and inspection. Many defects or problems – such as broken parts, flaws, or poorly fitting components – may be found through visual inspection. Sometimes an odd smell or sound may also alert people that there's a problem.

You may also be alerted to defects through delays. Delays are often early indications that something isn't right upstream. If ignored, they can cascade downstream and create significant backlogs. The third way you can detect problems is through changes in pattern. Lean processes are standardized, so they're highly patterned. Any disruption of a pattern is abnormal and may indicate a problem.

Inspection

In a jidoka system, all employees participate in checking quality at source – that is, they inspect pieces they receive before working on them, and inspect them again before passing them on, to check for any quality problems. In a factory that produces tables, for example, an employee notices a faulty weld on a metal table frame. So instead of proceeding to attach a wooden tabletop to the frame, the employee stops work and addresses the problem.

Delays

When a batch of units is late arriving at an employee's station in a production line, the employee investigates immediately. Similarly, when an employee in a government department receives a regular report from a team member half a day late, the employee follows up on the problem rather than ignoring it.

Changes in patterns

When a part, a trolley, or a person isn't in the right place at the right time, employees in a jidoka system assume there's a reason. Something isn't working as it should or according to pattern, and this calls for human attention.

As well as relying on employees, you can use automated mechanisms to detect errors. For example, you may install a device to identify any abnormalities in a product or process. This type of device is an example of a poka yoke. Poka yokes for detecting deviations or errors include different types of sensors. For example, computerized X-ray scanners can check the quality of welds in tin cans.

Many different kinds of detection poka yokes are used in manufacturing. When a piece is too light, too heavy, too hot or cold, too early or late, too large, misaligned, or misshaped, a poka yoke may alert an operator that something is wrong. A poka yoke may make a sound, flash a warning light, send a message to a phone, or simply stop an operation to alert the operator to a problem.

In a service industry or office environment, poka yoke mechanisms are often integrated into the computers or machines employees use. For example, computer software is designed to detect problems and alert users by triggering the display of error messages.

Question

Which are examples of poka yokes for detecting problems?

Options:

1. A unit that monitors the oil level in a machine, with an indicator light that flashes when the level drops too low

2. A sensor that alerts operators when the temperature of a fluid falls below a set threshold

3. Visual inspection of units by employees as they arrive at each station in a production process

4. Monitoring of any delays in the movement of units through a system by operators

Answer:

Option 1: This is a correct option. The indicator light in the unit is an automated measure to detect when the oil levels drop too low, which could potentially damage the machine irreparably. It is therefore an example of poka yoke.

Option 2: This is a correct option. The sensor alerts operators if the temperature of a substance drops to a level that requires the operator's machine to be serviced. This automated measure is an example of poka yoke.

Option 3: This is an incorrect option. A visual inspection is done manually and is therefore not an example of poka yoke, which is an automated mechanisms to detect errors.

Option 4: This is an incorrect option. When operators monitor delays, they do so manually. Poka yoke is an automated mechanisms to detect errors.

STOPPING AND FIXING THE PROBLEM

Stopping and fixing the problem

In jidoka, once you've detected the abnormality or problem, you stop the process. This is recommended whether you're working in a manufacturing or service environment.

Manufacturing

In a production setting, stopping a process involves literally stopping the production line so that the product under assembly can't advance. For example, a machine may shut down automatically because it has detected a fault, or someone may press a button to stop a conveyor belt.

Service

In an office setting, stopping a process could involve stopping whatever you are doing at your workstation. For example, you stop filling out a form when you notice the monthly sales totals are missing from the report you've been given, rather than continuing to work with the defective report.

Similarly, a software developer who is integrating graphics into a user manual and detects a flaw in the images should stop rather than integrating the flawed images.

Once you've stopped production, you fix the immediate problem in the short term. You do what it takes to get production flowing again. It's usually workers on the ground who perform this step. They'll pass the problem up the chain of command only if additional advice or assistance is required.

There are some common examples of immediate, short-term fixes to problems in a manufacturing setting:

- discarding a defective part and taking another from a bin,
- reworking a faulty unit,
- fixing a tool, and
- finding a quick way to bypass malfunctioning equipment.

In the service industry, an example of a quick fix might be obtaining information that was missing from a report from a different source.

If you need to complete a form, you might obtain missing information from another source, even if it takes a few minutes longer than normal, just so you can complete your work.

What's common to all the examples of fixes presented so far is that they don't address why the errors occurred in the first place. Instead, they're temporary countermeasures.

Question

After the immediate problem is fixed, the jidoka process continues with step 4 which involves installing a poka yoke or other measures. Do you think the following statement is true or false?

"The key difference between step 3 and step 4 is that step 3 inolves a temporary solution, where step 4 focuses on finding and implementing a permanent solution to prevent recurrence of the same problem."

Options:
1. True
2. False

Answer

Step 3 of the jidoka process is to fix the immediate problem. It provides only a temporary solution. Step 4 involves installing poka yoke or other measures to permanently solve a problem and prevent it from reoccurring.

INSTALLING A POKA YOKE

Installing a poka yoke

The final step in applying jidoka is to investigate the root cause of a problem and then to install a poka yoke – or take other measures – to prevent the problem from recurring.

Some types of problems can easily be prevented. For example, the root cause of a problem could be a faulty or worn piece of equipment or a worker who isn't using a specified process. The equipment can be replaced and the worker may be trained.

In other cases, problems might require more expensive or high-tech solutions. For example, electrical component and semi-conductor fabrication plants now stage much of the production process in cleanrooms, where dust and static electricity can be strictly controlled to prevent product defects or equipment failure.

For example, pharmaceutical manufacturing plants go through a very complex and difficult process to investigate and address the root causes of product contamination.

First they develop cleanroom production areas using high efficiency particulate air filters and ultraviolet lights.

When contamination remains a problem, cleanrooms are pressurized to prevent the inflow of air from outside. But this still allows contaminants to be tracked in by trolley wheels and foot traffic. So polymer floor mats are added to the cleanrooms. These actively attract contaminants through their yielding, mildly adhesive, and electrostatic properties, ensuring safety requirements are fully met.

Next consider an example in the service industry. The developer who noticed a flaw in the graphics finds that a specifications document lists the incorrect information for image resolution and color saturation. So an automated checklist is used to double-check specifications before the images are sent on to the developers.

So once you've identified the root cause of a problem, you take corrective action. This can involve installing a poka yoke or taking other defect prevention measures.

In manufacturing, for instance, corrective action could include printing "This side up" on cartons or using brush bristles that change color when they become worn. In the service industry, it may mean providing further training, using data entry software that won't allow users to advance to a new screen until required fields are completed, or changing a process.

Question

Sequence examples of activities that occur during the jidoka process.

Options:

A. The injection-molding machine flashes a red light

B. The operator switches off the injection-molding machine

C. The operator adds coolant to the machine

D. Engineers investigate why the machine overheats and install an automated cooling unit in it

Answer:

The injection-molding machine flashes a red light is ranked the first step.

The first step in the jidoka process is to detect the problem. In this case, the injection-molding machine automatically detects the problem and flashes a red light.

The operator switches off the injection-molding machine is ranked the second step.

The second step in the jidoka process is to stop the work process. The operator does this by switching off the injection-molding machine.

The operator adds coolant to the machine is ranked the third step.

The third step in the jidoka process is to fix the immediate problem. The operator realizes the machine is overheating and adds coolant as a temporary fix.

Engineers investigate why the machine overheats and install an automated cooling unit in it is ranked the fourth step.

The final step in jidoka is to investigate the root cause of the problem and, when possible, install a poka yoke – like a cooling unit that will kick in automatically when it's required – to prevent the problem from occurring again.

CHAPTER III - LEAN TOOLS AND TECHNIQUES FOR FLOW AND PULL

CHAPTER III - Lean Tools and Techniques for Flow and Pull
   SECTION 1 - Fundamentals of Lean: The Visual Workplace
   SECTION 2 - Fundamentals of Lean: Just-in-time
   SECTION 3 - Fundamentals of Lean: Kanban
   SECTION 4 - Fundamentals of Lean: Line Balancing

SECTION 1 - FUNDAMENTALS OF LEAN: THE VISUAL WORKPLACE

SECTION 1 - Fundamentals of Lean: The Visual Workplace

The visual workplace helps convey key information easily. This enables employees to complete their tasks safely and correctly. In turn, this reduces employee stress and improves morale.

The visual workplace tools available include work instructions, process flow diagrams, labels, andons, and status boards.

GOALS OF THE VISUAL WORKPLACE

Goals of the visual workplace

No doubt you've heard the expression "A picture is worth a thousand words." Sometimes information that may be difficult to explain clearly in words can be much more effectively conveyed through images. For example, is it easier to describe the Eiffel Tower in words or to show someone a photograph of it? The brain is able to process visual information very quickly. Careful use of visual cues can enable you to effectively communicate with your colleagues or customers.

Visual cues can come in many forms: warning signs, process flow charts, status charts, building maps, indication lights, colored labels, and simple arrows, for example. The key is to keep them simple, succinct, and effective.

If you apply Lean techniques when using visual cues, you'll be able to convey information in a way that saves time, energy, and money. Visual cues are more efficient because they can convey information quickly. And they reduce the need for repeated verbal messages or costly documentation.

In a Lean working environment, a workplace that effectively uses visual cues to convey information is called a "visual workplace." The visual workplace uses signs, layouts, charts, and color codes to inform employees and customers where things are, what the current status of projects are, and where there are possible dangers, among other things.

Time and resources can be wasted when people aren't able to find the resources they need to complete their tasks.

Waste can also be caused by people being unclear about their roles or responsibilities. Or it could be the result of errors and accidents caused by people not doing their tasks correctly. The visual workplace reduces waste by presenting information clearly and objectively. Depending on the industry you're in, you might either work in a visual office or a visual factory.

Visual office

The visual office is primarily used in service industries. It enables employees to see at a glance what their role is, how the office is organized, and whether the company or department is achieving its goals. For example, a call center would use visual cues such as pie charts and bar graphs to indicate how well it's achieving its customer service metrics.

Visual factory

The visual factory is primarily used in manufacturing industries. It enables management to immediately see the current status of all processes, and it enables employees to see the correct procedures to follow. This helps to reduce manufacturing errors and employee accidents. This in turn reduces waste and increases production. For example, a computer factory would use process diagrams to show employees how to complete production tasks effectively and safely.

The visual workplace can help companies achieve several goals:
- it ensures work is completed properly, safely, and on schedule,
- it ensures procedures are standardized and order is sustained, and
- it reduces employee stress and improves morale by providing them with the information they need when they need it.

A small bank guarantees its customers that its employees will answer customer phone calls promptly. However, the flow of customer queries to the bank's call center is unpredictable. The bank might receive a lot of calls in the last hour of business. Employees then find it difficult to cope with the volume of calls and have to work overtime to catch up on their other tasks.

The manager decides to monitor the calls more closely. She uses charts to post hourly updates on the average customer wait time. If the wait times are getting too long, the manager transfers more employees to concentrate on clearing the call backlog.

The manager places the charts in a prominent position in the office. The charts use large text and clear graphics so that employees can see at a glance what the average customer wait times are.

Question
What are the primary goals of the visual workplace?

Options:

1. To ensure work is completed properly, safely, and on schedule
2. To help standardize procedures
3. To reduce employee stress
4. To increase sales
5. To reduce inventory

Answer:

Option 1: This option is correct. The visual workplace makes it easier for employees to complete their tasks in a safe and efficient manner.

Option 2: This option is correct. The visual workplace results in a tidier, more organized workplace and aims to sustain these improvements.

Option 3: This option is correct. The visual workplace can reduce employee frustration and stress and improve morale.

Option 4: This option is incorrect. The main aim is to make the workplace more organized and efficient. This will help employees carry out their tasks more efficiently, but won't necessarily increase sales.

Option 5: This option is incorrect. The visual workplace aims to organize the workplace. Other Lean tools, such as just-in-time, are used to reduce inventory.

SELECTING VISUAL WORKPLACE TOOLS

Selecting visual workplace tools

The visual workplace isn't a "one size fits all" solution. It's a blend of tools and techniques that complement each other and help you create an efficient workplace.

By carefully studying the needs of your organization and your customers, you'll be able to select the visual tools that can best help you. There are a variety of tools to choose from:
- work instructions,
- process flow diagrams,
- labels,
- lights, commonly called andons, and
- status boards.

Work instructions, the first tool in the visual workplace, are short, simple guides on how to complete a specific task, such as how to replace a refrigerator light. They should be placed near to where a person would carry out that task. The instructions should be concise, easy to read, in clear font, and supported with simple illustrations if necessary.

You shouldn't use a lot of text in work instructions. Use visual directions – such as illustrations or photographs – where possible. Place the instructions where people can clearly see them. For example, a work instruction on how to change the toner in the office photocopier should be placed on the wall beside the copier, at the point of need.

Using work instructions helps ensure that tasks are completed correctly. This reduces the time lost to mistakes and accidents. The office employees at a busy travel agency have to fax many documents during the day. Select the problem and solution to learn more about the problem and how work instructions provided a solution.

Problem

Some employees are unsure of how to operate the fax machine. Faxes sometimes don't get transmitted, and employees waste time having to show others how to correctly use the machine.

Solution

The manager wants to reduce the time lost by these mistakes. He draws up a simple work instruction, outlining in simple steps how to send a fax. He posts it on the wall beside the fax machine. He also puts a small note on the fax machine itself: "If you're unsure of how to send a fax, please refer to the posted work instruction." Soon, everyone in the office is able to send faxes without any mistakes.

Process flow diagrams, the second tool in the visual workplace, show the correct sequence of steps in a process. This helps to ensure that all workers who carry out the same task do so in the same way. A flow diagram shows the steps from the start of the process to the end. It indicates what decisions have to be made at various stages.

By standardizing workflow, you can reduce errors and employee frustration. Staff will find it easier to complete their tasks when they know exactly what they have to do. Once you have standardized your workflow, create a clear process flow diagram and make it available to all relevant employees.

A graphic design department has been receiving a lot of customer complaints about the quality of its graphics. One customer recently canceled an order when he saw the initial graphic mockups. Select the problem and the solution to learn more about the problem and how work flow diagrams can provide a solution.

Problem

After investigating the problem, the manager realizes that not all designers are following the same graphic production process. Some are using outdated software programs. Others are submitting graphics to production without having them checked by the quality department.

Solution

In order to standardize graphic design production, the manager meets with the team leads to create some best practices. They develop a work flow diagram that will ensure all designers are following the same process. All designers get a copy of the process flow diagram to display in their cubicles.

Labels are the third tool in the visual workplace. You can use labels to identify equipment and materials. For example, in a factory, labels could be used to identify what the different levers on a machine operate. In an office, you might use labels to identify which departments different supplies belong to. This can ensure that time isn't wasted by employees looking for materials.

Employees in a doctor's office often find it difficult to locate files when they're needed. Select the problem and solution to learn more about the problem and how labeling provided a solution.

Problem

The office employs a lot of temporary contract workers, who are never sure where to return files after they've used them. It seems that only some employees know exactly where everything should go, but they don't share this information with others. All this confusion is starting to lead to conflict in the office. Also, patients have started to complain about the wait times created by the obvious lack of organization.

Solution

The manager invests in new storage shelves and filing cabinets. She then completes an inventory of all the information the office has on file, including patient details, employee details, and financial details. Each filing cabinet is then clearly labeled according to the information it contains. The cabinet drawers are also labeled. For example, one cabinet is labeled "Patient details," and the four drawers are labeled "A-G," "H-N," "O-S," and "T-Z" so that files can easily be organized alphabetically.

Andons are the fourth tool in the visual workplace. At its simplest, an andon light is a colored light used to convey information. For example, the colors on a traffic light tell you when to stop, slow down, and go. Andons can refer to any electronic signaling device that updates you on the status of a process or warns you of impending danger. Andons are used on highways to let you know about dangers or likely delays ahead. Airports use andons to update passengers about delays, departures, and arrivals.

Colored signals can be used to tell managers when performance is below average, at average, or above average. For example, call centers use andons to inform employees when there is a serious backlog of customers. Sometimes, andons include audio warnings, such as alarms or beeping sounds, as well as visual indicators.

A building supply yard sends materials to sites all over the state and is facing delays. Select the problem and solution to learn more about the problem and how andons can provide a solution.

Problem

When the yard is busy, there are over 20 forklifts loading supplies onto trucks. Because his clients are working to strict deadlines, the building supplier can't afford to have delays in his yard. If clients don't get their supplies on time, they'll likely find other suppliers. Delays can be caused by operators not realizing that the forklift is about to run out of fuel or break down.

Solution

The forklifts all have warning lights on their dashboards. However, in some forklifts, these aren't working correctly. These alert the operators to when a forklift is low on fuel or is likely to experience a mechanical fault. Lights also warn the operators when the load is too heavy for the forklift. Andons also ensure that the forklifts are operated safely. For example, when a forklift is in reverse, a white light displays and a buzzer sounds. A light and buzzer also remind the operator to put on the seatbelt. By checking all andons and fixing them as necessary, the company was able to improve the operation of the forklifts.

Status boards are the fifth tool in the visual workplace. They are used to update people about performance metrics and project status. Status boards might be electronic display units or simple whiteboards. They let employees know whether they're on target to meet their deliverables. For example, a courier service would use status boards to indicate how many packages were delivered within the agreed time period. A financial office might use status boards to indicate how many new mortgages have been approved each month.

All status boards have the same objective: they enable people to compare where they are with where they want to be. For example, managers can use them to determine if sales are on target. Human Resource departments can check whether employee turnover levels are cause for concern. Call centers can see whether customer complaints are greater or less than expected.

A company that produces hiking gear has recently seen a serious drop in sales. This decline in profits has been caused by a number of factors.

Problem

Many customers have been complaining about the poor quality of many of the products. Last year, the company failed to deliver a large order of hiking boots on time for one of its major clients. That client has since taken its business to another company. Additionally, some high-profile competitors have cornered most of the market, and other competitors are selling similar products at a cheaper price.

Solution

To help employees meet deadlines, the manager posts daily status boards for major projects. The company has invested in a major new advertising campaign to raise its profile in the market. The sales team is using status boards to monitor sales since the launch of the new campaign. The quality team is using status boards to measure the number of defects found and the level of customer complaints. And the procurement team is using status boards to monitor the cost of supplies.

Question

Match each visual workplace tool with an example of it.

Options:

A. Work instruction
B. Process flow diagram
C. Label
D. Andon
E. Status board

Targets:

1. Visual cue showing how to change a tire on a car
2. Visual cue showing the steps for updating reports
3. Visual cue showing which files belong to which department
4. Visual cue warning you when fuel levels are running low
5. Visual cue outlining the sales for each day of the week

Answer:

Work instructions outline how to complete a short, discrete task.

Process flow diagrams show the steps in a process.

Labels help employees easily identify the contents of a file or the purpose of a part.

Andons are colored lights that convey information.

Status boards enable you to determine at a glance whether your team is on target to meet its goals.

x

SECTION 2 - FUNDAMENTALS OF LEAN: JUST-IN-TIME

SECTION 2 - Fundamentals of Lean: Just-in-time

The just-in-time approach enables you to ensure that your supplies are closely linked to customer demand. You order only the supplies that are needed to meet customer orders. This reduces inventory, storage, and transportation costs. It also results in more efficient processes because no supplies are wasted.

In order to successfully implement just-in-time, you must have good communications with your customers, your suppliers, and your employees. And you need to establish a pull system for your supplies.

BENEFITS OF USING JUST-IN-TIME

Benefits of using just-in-time

When you're shopping, do you buy just enough supplies to last you for the next day or two? Or do you try to stock up for the next month? You might think that it's more efficient to stock up for the month. However, if you do this, you're likely to buy more supplies than you actually need, because you want to "be on the safe side." You then end up with crowded shelves.

If you've got too many products, some will probably expire before you can use them and you'll have to throw them out. So what seemed like an efficient plan actually costs you time and money in the end. The just-in-time approach to supplies helps to prevent overstocking. Rather than filling their warehouses with supplies that they might need, companies should aim to order only what they do need, when they need it.

This requires careful daily monitoring of supply needs and efficient, accurate ordering of replacements. Just-in-time ensures that organizations have exactly the right amounts of the right materials every day. Traditionally, inventory was regarded as an asset, regardless of whether it was used. Just-in-time applies Lean thinking to inventory management. The Lean view of inventory differs from the traditional view of inventory.

Traditional view

Some companies regard inventory as an asset. Supplies in warehouses are used to build products that will hopefully be sold to customers eventually. According to this view, inventory is adding value to the company and contributing to its profits.

Lean view

In a Lean environment, excess inventory is regarded as waste. Unused supplies have to be paid for and they lead to increased storage costs. By ordering more supplies than it needs, a company cuts into its profit margins. Also, excess supplies make it more difficult for employees to find the supplies they're looking for. This leads to wasted time and inefficient production.

Although just-in-time originated in the automobile industry, it has been implemented in many industries. In fact, any organization hoping to streamline its supply procurement process could benefit from just-in- time.

Manufacturing company

A manufacturing company can implement just-in-time in order to reduce the number of unused parts it has in storage.

Service company

A service company can use just-in-time to reduce infrastructure and resource costs. For example, there is no need for a large stationery room if you order letterhead, envelopes, and other office supplies as you need them.

By implementing just-in-time, a company can reduce costs associated with buying, transporting, and storing supplies.

The company can also become more productive. Companies have to make their processes more efficient because just-in-time doesn't allow much room for production mistakes. And the company's customers are more likely to be satisfied, as they'll receive high quality products in a timely fashion.

Question

How can implementing just-in-time benefit a company?

Options:

1. The company reduces costs
2. The company meets its goals
3. The company reduces wages
4. The company becomes more productive
5. The company increases customer satisfaction
6. The company widens its customer base

Answer:

Option 1: This option is correct. Just-in-time can reduce costs associated with buying, transporting, and storing supplies.

Option 2: This option is correct. By reducing costs, increasing production time, and improving quality, just-in-time enables companies to meet their goals.

Option 3: This option is incorrect. Just-in-time can improve employee morale by making workspaces tidier and more efficient. However, it doesn't reduce wage costs.

Option 4: This option is correct. Just-in-time doesn't allow much room for production mistakes, so companies have to make their processes more efficient.

Option 5: This option is correct. Quality is improved and production times are reduced. This leads to increased customer satisfaction because they get high quality goods when they want them.

Option 6: This option is incorrect. Just-in-time ensures that companies have the supplies needed for their current customer needs. Increasing sales is not a direct benefit of just-in-time.

IMPLEMENTING JUST-IN-TIME

Implementing just-in-time

Just-in-time is more than a few simple steps. It's a production philosophy that aims to reduce waste and increase value. It requires constant monitoring and continuous improvement. The driving force behind any just-in-time implementation is customer demand. As customers demand products, the necessary supplies are pulled into the system to meet those demands. The two keys to implementing just-in-time are good communication and establishing a pull system.

Communication is the first key to a successful just-in-time process. This involves good communication with customers, employees, and suppliers.

Customers

There must be clear communication between the company and its customers. The company needs to understand its customers' demands, needs, and quality expectations. It must find out what products customers want and when they want them, and then build those products.

Employees

Management must communicate the goals of just-in-time to all employees. A training program driven by management helps ensure that everyone knows the goals of the just-in-time program. And employees should be flexible as new processes are introduced.

Suppliers

Working closely with its suppliers ensures the correct amount of supplies arrive when needed. Supplies should be ordered based on customer demand. By communicating regularly with its suppliers, a company can ensure that it always has exactly the right supplies to meet its customers' needs. Where possible, companies should aim to use suitable suppliers who are close by. This helps to reduce transport costs and enables good communication.

Question

What are some of the steps you can take to ensure successful implementation of just-in-time?

Options:

1. Always choose the cheapest suppliers
2. Communicate just-in-time goals to all employees
3. Communicate regularly with suppliers
4. Choose suppliers who are close by
5. Communicate with customers after production
6. Find out when customers want products

Answer:

Option 1: This option is incorrect. The cheapest supplier isn't always the best one. Aim for suppliers who are reliable and who can deliver high quality goods.

Option 2: This option is correct. Employees must get behind the just-in-time strategy, so you need to communicate the goals clearly to them.

Option 3: This option is correct. Regular communication is a key element of an effective just-in-time process.

Option 4: This option is correct. Choosing suppliers who are close by can reduce transport costs. Option 5: This option is incorrect. You must communicate with customers regularly before and during production to make sure you understand their needs.

Option 6: This option is correct. It's not enough to know what products customers want. You also need to know when they want them.

Manufacturing processes can be understood as being either push or pull. Establishing a pull process is the second key to establishing just-in-time.

In the "push" process, supplies are pushed through the system based on estimated product demand. A company accumulates a large stock of supplies and then builds the products. Employees are never idle because they're working on products regardless of real customer demand. As a result, the company may build more products than it can sell. This leads to increased storage costs and reduced profits.

In the "pull" process, supplies are pulled through the system, based on actual product demand. No product is built until there's a definite need for it. The company doesn't accumulate large supply reserves. Instead, it fulfills smaller orders on an as-needed basis. This results in reduced costs and more efficient processes. It also helps ensure that the company doesn't build products that it can't sell – processes answer the pull of customer demand.

In a just-in-time system, levels of inventory are based on actual need. You can use kanban cards to monitor actual need. Kanban cards are signals that more supplies are needed. New supplies aren't ordered until the kanban card signifies a need for them.

Question

Which steps should you take to establish a pull system for your just-in-time process?

Options:

1. Build up a reserve of inventory so that employees aren't idle

2. Adjust processes so that you build products based on actual customer demand

3. Use kanban cards to signal the need for new supplies

4. Increase your storage space so you are better able to meet potential customer demand

Answer:

Option 1: This option is incorrect. One of the key aims of just-in-time is reducing inventory.

Option 2: This option is correct. Just-in-time is based on meeting actual customer demand, rather than estimates and forecasts.

Option 3: This option is correct. Supplies aren't ordered until a kanban card signals that they're needed.

Option 4: This option is incorrect. A pull system enables you to reduce your storage space by eliminating unwanted supplies.

An electronics company produces radios for the home entertainment market. Business has been brisk for a number of years, but recently sales have stalled. The company plans its production schedule in January and factory employees have been working toward these targets. When sales start to decline, the company discovers that it's producing more radios than it can sell. The company decides to implement just-in-time to address this problem.

Company management consults with the sales team to get a more accurate picture of actual sales. They ask the sales team to provide monthly updates on current sales. Armed with this information, the managers meet with the company's suppliers in the next city. They set up a monthly supply system, so that each month's supplies are more closely aligned to current sales figures. As sales decrease, the orders for parts and supplies also decrease.

Management also meets with employees. They stress that radios would no longer be produced unless there's a definite need for them. This means that some employees might be deployed to other projects when demand for radios was low.

Establish communication

The company established good communication with its suppliers, customers, and employees.

Establish a pull system

By getting a clearer idea of customer demand, the company was able to establish a pull system. Radios would be built based on customer demand. This process could be improved by introducing kanban cards for supplies. This would help make the pull system more efficient.

Now consider this non-manufacturing example. A hotel uses an online system to manage its reservations and prides itself on meeting customer demand. It ensures that there's enough food in the kitchens for the breakfast and lunchtime rush. By forecasting customer demand, it orders supplies based on these estimates. However, sometimes the estimates are inaccurate and the kitchen ends up throwing out a lot of food.

Because of the cost of all this wasted food, management decides to implement just-in-time. It wants the food supply orders to be more closely linked to the actual reservations, rather than forecasts.

The general manager uses the hotel's online reservations system to generate accurate reports on the number of guests in the hotel each week. He then passes this information on to the kitchen supplies manager.

The kitchen supplies manager meets with the local suppliers to agree on a more flexible approach to supply ordering. Rather than ordering the same amount of food each week, the hotel lets the supplier know that the order will change from week to week.

Establish communication

The hotel established an effective communication system. Its online reservation system enables customers to communicate with the hotel. And the hotel has set up a good system for communicating with its suppliers. Using local suppliers also ensures the hotel can keep transport costs to a minimum.

Establish a pull system

The hotel established an effective pull system. Less food is now wasted because supplies are ordered based on the pull of customer demand. Introducing kanban cards would make the system even better. The cards would help the kitchen supplies manager monitor when new supplies are needed.

Case Study: Question 1 of 2

Scenario

For your convenience, the case study is repeated with each question.

A computer manufacturer has started implementing just-in-time in order to reduce inventory costs. The company's managers meet with the sales team every week to get an accurate picture of customer demand. The manufacturer uses an overseas supplier to provide cheap computer parts. Managers hold a conference call with the supplier every four months. A new kanban system has enabled the company to monitor its supplies.

Answer the questions, in order, to assess how the company is implementing just-in-time.

Question

What are the key components of a successful implementation of just-in-time?

Options:

1. Good communication with employees, suppliers, and customers
2. A pull system for ordering supplies
3. Extra storage space
4. Cheap suppliers

Answer:

Option 1: This option is correct. Communication enables a company to understand its customers' needs. Employees and suppliers can then work to meet these needs.

Option 2: This option is correct. Supplies should be ordered based on the pull of customer demand.

Option 3: This option is incorrect. The aim of just-in-time is to reduce storage space.

Option 4: This option is incorrect. The cheapest supplier is not always the best choice.

Case Study: Question 2 of 2

What steps should the computer manufacturer take to ensure the success of its just-in-time strategy?

Options:

1. Consider using more local suppliers
2. Meet with the sales team more often
3. Improve how it signals the need for new supplies
4. Improve communication with the supplier

Answer:

Option 1: This option is correct. Using local suppliers might reduce transport costs and improve communication.

Option 2: This option is incorrect. Meeting with the sales team every week should give the company an accurate picture of customer demand. This demand will form the basis of the pull system.

Option 3: This option is incorrect. Using kanban cards is the ideal way to signal the need for new supplies.

Option 4: This option is correct. The company should communicate more regularly with its suppliers.

SECTION 3 - FUNDAMENTALS OF LEAN: KANBAN

SECTION 3 - Fundamentals of Lean: Kanban

A kanban system is used to signal a need for supplies. This helps improve process efficiency because supplies aren't pulled into the system until a kanban card triggers a need. Kanban follows four rules. Downstream processes may only withdraw items as specified on the kanban. Upstream processes may only send items downstream as specified by the kanban. Defective parts can't be sent into the process and a kanban must accompany each item.

To implement a kanban system, you first conduct a supply survey and establish maximum and minimum levels. You then create a supply order form and kanban cards. Finally, you establish standard work and ensure all employees are trained on the new process.

RULES FOR KANBAN

Rules for kanban

How can you ensure that your processes run smoothly? Having the necessary supplies is one essential component. In an effective process, supplies are always available when they're needed. If you have too few supplies, production and services can grind to a halt. If you have too many supplies, your systems might become clogged up. By knowing exactly when new parts or supplies are needed, you can keep your processes running smoothly.

Kanban is a signaling system used to indicate what supplies or parts are required and when they're required. By knowing exactly when to send supplies, you can reduce your inventory and transport costs. You don't order a part until you receive a signal that the part is needed.

The kanban is the signal you use to indicate that a new part is needed. The signal might be a card, for example. Each part might have a kanban card attached to it. When the part is used, the card is detached and sent to the supply manager. The supply manager then knows to send on a new part.

Note

"Kanban" in Japanese means "a card you can see."

An effective kanban system follows four rules:
- downstream processes may only withdraw items in the precise amounts specified on the kanban,
- upstream processes may only send items downstream in the precise amounts that have been withdrawn, which are specified by the kanban,
- defective parts or incorrect amounts are never sent to the next downstream process, and
- a kanban must accompany each item at all times.

In modern mass production plants, kanbans no longer take the form of cards in a bin.

Instead, they're messages sent from one computer to another computer via kanban software. This then triggers the replenishment of supply chambers. However, the principle of pull production is still behind the system.

Question

What are the four rules for implementing a kanban process?

Options:

1. Downstream processes may only withdraw items in the precise amounts specified on the kanban

2. Upstream processes may only send items downstream in the precise amounts that have been withdrawn, which are specified by the kanban

3. Defective parts or incorrect amounts are never sent to the next downstream process

4. A kanban must accompany each item at all times

5. Kanbans can be sent only at the end of the day

6. You can send only one kanban per shift

Answer:

Option 1: This option is correct. You can withdraw no more or no fewer items than are specified on the kanban.

Option 2: This option is correct. This ensures that new items are added to the process in the rate that they're needed.

Option 3: This option is correct. If there are any flaws with a part, it can't be sent into the process.

Option 4: This option is correct. A kanban must accompany each item at all times. No items are made or moved without a kanban.

Option 5: This option is incorrect. The aim of kanbans is to signal exactly when new parts are needed. As soon as there's a need, you send a kanban.

Option 6: This option is incorrect. A kanban must be sent every time new supplies or parts are needed.

IMPLEMENTING KANBANS

Implementing kanbans

An effective kanban system enables you to ensure that you know immediately when to order new supplies. New orders are pulled by the demand for supplies.

Implementing a kanban system involves five steps:
- conduct a survey of your supplies,
- establish minimum and maximum levels you require to sustain production,
- create a supply order form for each part or material,
- create the kanban system, and
- establish standard work for how to use the kanban system and train employees.

Conduct a survey

Find out what supplies and parts your department or organization needs in order to function effectively. Detail the sizes and quality of the supplies needed. For example, your department might need 500 3/4 inch lug nuts. Or your office might need five boxes of A4 copy paper.

Establish minimum and maximum levels

What is the minimum number of this part you need in order to meet customer demand? When supplies go below this level, you have to reorder. Take into account variations in need and use. Establish a maximum supply level as well to avoid surplus inventory.

Create a supply order form

Creating a supply order form ensures a consistent approach to supply ordering. The form must state the exact number of supplies or parts required.

Create a kanban system

Use different colored cards for different types of supplies. For example, machine parts might use yellow cards, office supplies might use red cards, and so on. When the card is completed, it signals that new supplies have to be ordered. If there's no card, no supplies are ordered.

Establish standard work

A new system will work only if it's applied consistently. Create a standard work chart and make it available to all employees. For example, you might post the standard work chart beside the supply cabinet. And provide any necessary training in the new process. This helps ensure that the new improved process becomes standard work practice.

Now that you've explored the steps of the kanban process, consider the following example. An office manager is concerned about the cost of supplies. The last box of paperclips was taken a week ago, and no one has ordered more. When the printer ran out of paper, someone ordered ten boxes of paper. Now, people are tripping over the boxes. One box contains photo paper, which no one ever uses. And the office is always short of black and red pens, but has over 100 green ones.

Conduct a survey

By monitoring usage over a two-week period, the manager is able to identify what supplies are actually needed by the office. He discovers that everyone prefers using black and blue pens. Also, the office needs four boxes of paperclips. The manager then creates a checklist of the supplies needed for the office.

Establish minimum and maximum levels

By monitoring usage, the manager can establish accurate minimum and maximum levels. For example, the office always needs at least one box of printer paper, but never needs to have more than four.

Create a supply order form

To ensure consistent ordering, the manager creates a new supply order form. From now on, only the exact number of supplies required will be ordered.

Create the kanban system

If there is only one box of paper in the supply cabinet, a kanban card triggers a new order. The card is attached to the last box in the cabinet. The card specifies exactly how many boxes to order. This means that there will never be more boxes than needed in the cabinet.

Establish standard work

The manager decides to try out the new system for a month. He is delighted with the results and decides to make it standard practice, so he posts a standard work chart beside the supplies cabinet. All employees now know the correct procedure for ordering new supplies.

The office manager's new kanban system brought about a number of benefits:

- it reduced the cost of supplies, because no unnecessary supplies were ordered,
- it created a tidier office, because no space was taken up by unwanted supplies, and
- it improved productivity and morale, because all employees had the supplies they needed to do their jobs.

Now, examine how kanban is used in a manufacturing setting. The manager of a toy factory has noticed that the flow of supplies doesn't always match the flow of production. Although there's always enough inventory in the warehouse, there isn't always enough on the factory floor. For example, some workers don't have enough motors to assemble their products, but others have too many.

Conduct a survey

The manager decides to create a checklist of the supplies needed to create the toys. For example, most of the toys have a small motor. The manager wants to ensure that there are always enough motors on the factory floor for staff to make the toys. The manager then lists the other supplies needed, such as toy parts, paint, packaging, and so on.

Establish minimum and maximum levels

In order to keep production flowing, workers need to have at least five motors on their desks at any time. However, if they have more than eight motors, their desks become too cluttered.

Create a supply order form

The manager now has an accurate idea of the amount of supplies needed. He is then able to create a supply order form that will meet the needs of production.

Create the kanban system

The manager then creates the kanban system. As soon as a worker has fewer than six motors, he issues a kanban asking for three new motors. Workers can't issue a kanban until they have fewer than six motors.

Establish standard work

After trying out the new process for two weeks, the manager standardizes it and trains all employees on how to use it.

Case Study: Question 1 of 3

Scenario

A company that produces custom-made clothes has been very busy lately. And because it has been so busy, things have begun to get disorganized on the assembly line. Staff members are complaining that they can't meet production targets because they don't always have the materials needed to assemble the clothes.

Help the company implement a kanban system by answering the questions in order.

Question

What are the first two steps the production manager should take in order to implement a kanban system?

Options:

1. Consult with the sales department to find out what the customer demand is likely to be

2. Conduct a survey to determine the materials needed to make the clothes

3. Work out what the maximum and minimum levels of materials are

4. Put in place a kanban system

Answer:

Option 1: This option is incorrect. Kanban aims to ensure that workers always have the supplies they need.

Option 2: This option is correct. The first step in implementing a kanban system is to conduct a survey of your supplies.

Option 3: This option is correct. The second step in implementing a kanban system is to establish the maximum and minimum levels of supplies needed to keep production flowing.

Option 4: This option is incorrect. The manager shouldn't create the kanban cards until there's a better idea of the supplies that are needed for production and what quantities should be on hand.

Case Study: Question 2 of 3

The manager dicovers that each clothing worker has a bin that holds up to 220 buttons. Supplies must be replenished when the bin reaches 20 buttons remaining for the work to be continued without disruption.

What steps should the manager take next in order to implement the kanban system?

Options:

1. Order 200 buttons to be sent to the workers when their bins have 20 or fewer buttons remaining

2. Reduce inventory by reducing the number of buttons needed for each item of clothing

3. Find suppliers who can reduce the cost of buttons and materials

4. Create the kanban card for new buttons

Answer:

Option 1: This option is correct. The manager must put in place a consistent system for ordering supplies.

Option 2: This option is incorrect. The kanban system doesn't aim to change production processes. Instead, it aims to ensure the production processes always have the supplies they need.

Option 3: This option is incorrect. A kanban system may lead to reduced inventory costs by more efficient management of supplies. However, finding new suppliers isn't an aim of the kanban system.

Option 4: This option is correct. New supplies of buttons are sent to the production line only when the kanban card signals a need. This ensures employees never have too few or too many supplies.

Case Study: Question 3 of 3

It's becoming obvious to the manager that the kanban system is bringing benefits. Employees are never short of parts and the work areas are much tidier than before.

What final steps should the manager take to ensure the success of the new system?

Options:

1. Establish standard work documents and procedures for ordering materials

2. Check to see whether sales of clothes are increasing under the new system

3. Set up a program to train employees in the new system

4. Check the quality of incoming supplies

Answer:

Option 1: This option is correct. The improved system must become the new way of doing things. When the new process is agreed on and documented, it can become standard practice.

Option 2: This option is incorrect. Kanban is a supply management system. Profits might increase because of more efficient inventory control. However, increased sales isn't an aim of the kanban system.

Option 3: This option is correct. The new system will succeed only if employees get behind it. They must understand how the kanban system works and what benefits it'll bring.

Option 4: This option is incorrect. Kanban aims to ensure employees always have the supplies they need to carry out their tasks. However, the kanban system doesn't monitor the quality of supplies. Other Lean tools are used to do this.

SECTION 4 - FUNDAMENTALS OF LEAN: LINE BALANCING

SECTION 4 - Fundamentals of Lean: Line Balancing

Line balancing enables you to distribute work evenly among your employees. It ensures that no workers are overburdened or underburdened. In an ideal situation, the pace of production matches the pace of customer demand. By calculating the takt time, you can tell if your line is balanced with the right number of workers.

GOALS OF LINE BALANCING

Goals of line balancing

In any process, one of your key aims is to distribute the work evenly and efficiently. If one worker is overburdened, this causes delays in the entire process. Because of the delay, the next workers are then overburdened when the work reaches them. How can you avoid this problem? By using line balancing to optimally distribute the work among your team. This in turn helps to reduce manpower requirements and costs.

In an assembly line, the work might be balanced or unbalanced among employees.

Unbalanced

In an unbalanced line, work is distributed unevenly across the line. This leads to bottlenecks in the process, with resulting delays, costs, and employee frustration. Some employees are overworked and others are left waiting for the work to come to them. If employees at stage 2 of the process are overworked, employees at stages 3 and 4 are going to be delayed. Some will end up doing overtime, while others are wasting time.

Balanced

In a balanced line, work is distributed evenly across the line. Each employee completes the same amount of work in roughly the same amount of time. This prevents delays and promotes continuous workflow.

Line balancing aims to achieve two main goals:
- to distribute work evenly among workers, and
- to ensure that you have the optimal number of workers.

Distribute work evenly

When you distribute work evenly among workers, you can eliminate bottlenecks and wait time. This ensures that no workers are too busy or idle.

Have optimal number

When you have the optimal number of workers, production neither exceeds nor fails to meet customer demand.

Now that you've learned about line balancing, consider this example. A company produces small digital cameras. It has workers dedicated to different tasks along its assembly line. Some employees are involved in assembling the cameras, some test the cameras, and some package them. The production manager is worried because the company is always falling behind its production targets. There are simply too many bottlenecks in the process.

After carefully studying the production flow, the manager realizes that the camera testers can't keep up with the rate of production. Too many cameras are coming off the assembly line for them to handle.

This means that the packers are also delayed as they wait for the testers to complete their tasks. Packers are sometimes standing around for an hour waiting for the cameras to arrive.

The production manager decides to move some workers from the assembly line to the testing line, since similar skills were needed for both lines. This helps balance the workload between the two lines. The testers are now able to keep pace with production. And the packers have a steady flow of cameras to package.

The camera factory achieved a number of goals by implementing line balancing.

Distribute work evenly

The production manager was able to divide the work evenly among the assemblers, testers, and packers. This meant no one was overburdened or underburdened. Because no workers are overburdened, there are no bottlenecks in the process. This also avoids delays further down the line.

Have optimal number

By studying the production flow, the manager was able to place the optimal number of workers at each stage. This ensured production flowed smoothly.

Line balancing can be used in offices as well as factories. For example, in a financial call center, the customer service agents guide customers through the fulfillment process. The process begins when the customer calls the agent and requests a new line of credit. The agent enters the customer's personal information and other relevant data into the computer.

An enterprise management system submits the request to the relevant department or person. The request is then processed. If the request is approved, the loan agreement and other necessary documentation are sent to the customer. The fulfillment process ends with the customer receiving the line of credit. Line balancing helped the call center achieve a number of goals.

Distribute work evenly

With line balancing, calls are evenly distributed among customer service agents. They can be filtered based on the nature of the call, for example. Because work is evenly distributed, there are no bottlenecks. No one is overburdened, so applications don't become backlogged.

Have optimal number

Line balancing enables the manager to ensure the right number of agents are available to meet the demand.

Remember you may have to rebalance your lines to accommodate periods of peak customer demand. For example, a restaurant would have to redistribute its workload at lunchtime. A hotel would redistribute its workload during vacation season. A toy factory would redistribute its workload in the run up to the holiday season.

Question

What are the primary goals of line balancing?

Options:

1. To distribute work evenly among workers, thus eliminating bottlenecks and wait time
2. To reduce inventory
3. To ensure you have the optimal number of workers
4. To ensure work is always balanced at the same levels

Answer:

Option 1: This option is correct. By distributing work evenly among workers, you can eliminate the bottlenecks that negatively affect process efficiency.

Option 2: This option is incorrect. Line balancing is mainly concerned with workers, rather than supplies and inventory.

Option 3: This option is correct. When you have the optimal number of workers, production neither exceeds nor fails to meet customer demand.

Option 4: This option is incorrect. Lines may have to be rebalanced at certain times to meet customer demand.

USING TAKT TIME

Using takt time

One of the goals of line balancing is to ensure that work is evenly distributed among workers. In the ideal state, each worker spends roughly the same amount of time on similar tasks. This ideal processing time is known as "takt time."

Takt time is the work rate needed to meet customer demand. In an effective process, the rate of production matches the rate of demand. In other words, production responds to the pull of customer demand. Knowing the takt time enables you to accurately pace your production. The pace of production must be in sync with the pace of sales.

To calculate the takt time, you first must know the available work time. Say your employees work an 8- hour day, but take 1 1/2 hours for lunch and breaks. The available work time is then 6 1/2 hours, or 390 minutes. You then divide the available work time by the customer demand, which in this case is 3 products every day. The takt time is then 390 divided by 3, or 130 minutes per product.

The customer service agents in the financial call center are under pressure to keep up with customer demand. In order to better manage the work flow, the manager decides to calculate the takt time for the call center. The manager must first calculate the available work time. The office is open for 8 hours each day, with each employee having a half-hour lunch break and two 15 minute breaks. So the available work time is 7 hours, or 420 minutes.

The second step is to calculate customer demand. On average, each employee receives 240 customer queries per day. To calculate the takt time, the manager divides the available work time by the customer demand. 420 minutes divided by 240 customer queries gives a takt time of 1.75 minutes, or 1 minute 45 seconds per customer query.

If production or service time rise above takt time, your company will not be able to keep up with customer demand. For example, say the financial call center is answering one customer query every 3 minutes and takt time is 1 minute 45 seconds.

This will result in complaints from customers. Also, it may lead to employees working overtime to clear the backlog, which is likely to lead to discontent. Also, costs are likely to increase, as you have to pay employees extra for the overtime. If production or service time is faster than takt time, you're working faster than is necessary to meet customer demand. Say the call center is answering one customer query every minute. That means that at times, agents will be idle.

In a manufacturing situation, if your workers produce faster than takt time, you end up with a product surplus. This is a waste of resources and money. Whether workers are working below takt time, or exceeding takt time, the solution is the same: balance the line so that you have the optimal number of workers working just to takt time.

Question

A furniture company must produce a hand-made sofa every 2 hours in order to meet customer demand. Given the information in the chart, what problem is the company likely to face in the future? The takt time is 120 minutes. Worker time is 110 minutes.

Options:

1. The company is unlikely to be able to meet customer demand

2. The company is likely to have products that it can't sell

3. The workers aren't working fast enough

Answer:

Option 1: This option is incorrect. To meet customer demand, the workers should be taking 120 minutes to produce each sofa. Because employees are working faster than takt time, the company is actually exceeding customer demand.

Option 2: This is the correct option. Employees are working faster than takt time. Therefore, production is rushing ahead of customer demand.

Option 3: This option is incorrect. The workers are working 10 minutes faster than takt time. They're actually working too fast compared to customer demand.

CHAPTER IV - REDUCING WASTE AND STREAMLINING VALUE FLOW USING LEAN

CHAPTER IV - Reducing Waste and Streamlining Value Flow Using Lean
    SECTION 1 - Value-add and Non-value-add Activities
    SECTION 2 - Muda and the Seven Wastes
    SECTION 3 - Continuous Flow and Line Balancing

SECTION 1 - VALUE-ADD AND NON-VALUE-ADD ACTIVITIES

SECTION 1 - Value-add and Non-value-add Activities

In a Lean approach, value-add activities meet customers needs or preferences, change the product or service, and are done right the first time. Activities that don't meet these criteria are non-value-add activities and, when possible, should be eliminated.

However, some non-value-add activities are necessary for business operation or to meet regulatory or accreditation standards. These are classified as required non-value-add activities. The goal should be to minimize the cost and effort of performing these activities.

CRITERIA FOR VALUE-ADD ACTIVITIES

Criteria for value-add activities

Each person in an organization values different things. So it can be difficult figuring out what's wasteful and what's useful for the organization. Lean provides clear guidelines on this. It makes it simple to define what's valuable for a business and what constitutes waste.

According to Lean, value is a rating of how well a product or service meets a customer's requirements. If it's something a customer is willing to pay for, it has value. The different activities performed during a process either add value to the end product or they don't. So activities can be either value-add or non-value-add.

Value-add

Value-add activities make a product or service more valuable from a customer's point of view. For example, connecting components, polishing a completed product, and delivering the product to a customer are value-add activities.

Non-value-add

Non-value-add activities don't add any extra value to the end product or service from the customer's perspective. For example, transporting components and conducting inspections are non-value-add activities.

Consider this example of a value-add activity. By slicing bread before offering it for sale, an enterprising baker adds a step that makes using bread more convenient for customers. Customers become more willing to buy it. Any procedure a customer is willing to pay for adds value.

It's likely that every procedure a company implements seems valuable to someone. For example, managers may value long, thorough hiring interviews. The interviews may have value for people inside the company and may also be necessary for hiring the right people for the company. However, customers may not be willing to pay for these procedures. So according to a Lean perspective, hiring interviews don't add value.

To determine if a procedure or activity adds value, you need to be able to answer "Yes" to three questions – Does it fulfill a customer's need or preference? Does it change the product or service in some way? Is it done right the first time in the process?

When workers install bolts to attach a handle to a product, they're fulfilling a customer's need for a handle on the product. Customers expect to pay the cost of assembling the product and want handles, so this procedure adds value. Similarly, entering data from invoices and receipts into an accounting system adds value because customers need to be able to balance their books.

Inspections catch many errors that would disappoint customers. However, customers rarely know or care whether a product has been inspected a dozen times or not at all. They simply expect the product to work to their satisfaction as was promised by the sales people. So the procedure for conducting inspections doesn't itself add value.

Installing a spark plug in an automobile engine or cooking a hamburger makes a physical change in the item that becomes a finished product. So these activities are performed to add value.

Similarly, a programmer who writes computer instructions or a banker who negotiates the interest on a loan is acting in a way that makes a change in a service, even if the change can't be seen.

In an office setting, making and storing extra copies of documents doesn't change the service provided. So this activity doesn't add value. In Lean, activities focused on getting things right the first time add value. For example, using poka yoke – which are mechanisms that automatically prevent or correct errors as they occur – can add value by improving the quality of a product for customers.

Activities that involve finding or correcting mistakes only after they've been made aren't value-adding. For example, a customer who buys a television set won't find the product more valuable because the company that built it needed more than one try to get the wiring right.

Question

Your company has created a software application for a government agency. The agency now requires that you run specific tests on the software and document the results for meeting an important accreditation standard.

Do you think that this process is value-adding?

Options:

1. Yes
2. No
3. Unsure

Answer:

Option 1: Actually, you can't say "yes" to all three criteria for this process. Although it meets customer preferences and may be done right the first time, it doesn't change the end product. So using the strict definition, testing and documenting the results aren't value-add activities. However, the process is required.

Option 2: Although the process is required, it doesn't change the end product. So using the strict definition, it doesn't add value.

Option 3: The testing and documenting activities meet customer requirements and may be done right the first time. However, they won't change the end product. So although the process is required, it isn't value-adding.

Question

Which criteria do value-add activities meet?

Options:

1. They fulfill a customer's needs or preferences
2. They change the product or service in some way
3. They're done right the first time
4. They're inexpensive to complete
5. They ensure products and services are inspected before delivery to customers

Answer:

Option 1: This option is correct. Any activity that a customer is willing to pay for or that meets the customer's requirements adds value if it also changes the product or service and is done right first time.

Option 2: This is a correct option. Any activity that changes the product or service into a more complete or desirable state adds value if it also fulfills customer requirements and is done right first time.

Option 3: This option is correct. Activities or procedures that are done right first time, that meet customer needs, and that change the product or service add value.

Option 4: This option is incorrect. The costs of activities don't determine whether they add value to a product or service for customers.

Option 5: This is an incorrect option. Inspections are actually non-value-add activities. Customers are likely to value high-quality products or services, but don't generally know or care whether they've been inspected. Also, if a process is completed right the first time, the need for inspections is reduced.

CLASSIFYING PRODUCTION ACTIVITIES

Classifying production activities

Not all activities that fail to meet the value-adding criteria should be scrapped. Some non-value-add activities are necessary even if they don't change a product or service, meet customer preferences, or ensure the task is completed right the first time. Non-value-add activities may be necessary to operate a business, or when you need to meet regulatory or accreditation standards that apply to your organization.

These types of activities are known as required non-value-add activities. For example, writing a production report, paying wages, or even implementing a Lean initiative are necessary for the efficient running of a business, even though they add no direct value for the customer. Typically, quality inspections are required non-value-add activities. At least one quality inspection should be performed before a product is delivered to the customer as a risk management strategy.

However, redundant or excessive quality checks don't add value and aren't required. Business support departments – such as HR, IT, Finance, and Legal departments – typically provide required non-value-add services. An organization's goal should be to minimize the effort needed to provide these services.

For example, the payroll service ensures employees receive the correct salaries on specified dates. This service is necessary for maintaining a workforce. So although it doesn't specifically add value, it can't be scrapped. However, an organization can reduce the costs, time, and effort associated with providing the payroll service. For example, it may do this by using payroll software to automate many tasks, and by using card scans and automatic check writers.

Question

In a scenario described earlier in the topic, an agency required that you run specific tests on software developed for a government agency and document the results.

Do you think that this is a required non-value-add procedure?

Options:
1. Yes
2. No

Answer:

Option 1: This is the correct option. The agency will accept the product only once the tests and documentation have been completed. So although these activities don't add value, they're required.

Option 2: This option is incorrect. The agency requires the tests and documentation. So although they don't add value, they're required.

By identifying value from the perspective of the customer, you can gain a fresh view of what it is that your organization actually does. You can then optimize value-add activities, minimize or remove non- value-add activities, and modify required non-value-add activities so they use less resources.

An insurance company wants to eliminate waste and add value to its processes and procedures. For the company, an example of a value-add activity is creating modular packages to meet the different needs of its customers. Making hard-copy backups of contracts and other documents, and having employees walking to the filing rooms to retrieve these documents, is non-value-adding. However, maintaining the document copies is regarded as a necessary precaution for the business.

To minimize the effort expended on backing up data, the company automates the process of copying electronic versions of files. The file backups are then instantly sent to an Internet-based storage hold and employees can access the data copies from their computers.

Question

A Lean team at a frozen foods factory is assessing the factory's activities and processes.

Match examples of activities to their types. More than one example may match a single category.

Options:

A. Slice raw vegetables into bite-sized pieces

B. Cook raw vegetables in a steam chamber

C. Calibrate steam chamber to meet food regulation standards

D. Transport food to a freezing area

E. Calibrate slicing machines to cut vegetables to the desired size

F. Inspect packaging to ensure the company logo is correctly displayed

Targets:
1. Value-add activities
2. Non-value-add activities
3. Required non-value-add activities

Answer:
Slicing and cooking the vegetables are value-add activities. They're done only once and change the product, providing the preferred bite-sized and pre-cooked vegetables that customers want.

Transporting food and inspecting packaging for marketing purposes are non-value-add activities. They don't change the product and aren't required for business operation or to meet regulations.

Calibrating the slicing and steaming machinery are required to ensure the factory meets regulations and for its basic operation, but they don't change the product. So they're required non-value-add activities.

SECTION 2 - MUDA AND THE SEVEN WASTES

SECTION 2 - Muda and the Seven Wastes

The seven categories of waste are overproduction, excess inventory and motion, transportation, waiting, overprocessing, and defects. Knowing typical causes of these wastes can help you assess underlying problems and find appropriate solutions.

IDENTIFYING WASTE

Identifying waste

To eliminate waste in your organization, you need to be able to recognize it and understand its causes. A good place to begin is adopting a clear definition of what waste is. In Lean, waste is defined as any use of resources that goes beyond what a customer requires and is willing to pay for.

Taiichi Ohno was the founder of the Toyota Production System on which Lean is based. He carefully reviewed processes and resource use for examples of waste. Based on his observations, he identified seven forms of waste. These forms of waste – also known as muda – are overproduction, overprocessing, motion, waiting, transportation, inventory, and defects.

Overproduction

Overproduction is the creation of more products, services, or components than either the operator at the next stage in the line of production or an external customer need.

Overprocessing

Overprocessing is applying more processes than needed to create a product, service, or component. Typically this includes using overly large, complex equipment or extra reworking in a process.

Motion

Motion refers to how employees are required to move while creating a product or providing a service.

Waiting

Equipment or employees may waste time waiting for another process to be completed before performing a task.

Transportation

Transportation is the movement of a product or its components. All transportation, other than delivery of a product to the customer, is considered waste.

Inventory

Inventory is material that is not yet needed and so must be stored. It may originate from suppliers or be the result of overproduction.

Defects

Defects are flaws in a product or service. A defect causes the product to either be discarded or reworked, and so represents waste.

Question

Match the seven types of wastes to their definitions.

Options:

A. Transportation
B. Motion
C. Overproduction
D. Inventory
E. Overprocessing
F. Waiting

Targets:

1. The movement of products or components
2. The movement of employees
3. The creation of inventory or unneeded products, components, or features
4. Material that is not yet needed
5. Using overly large or complex equipment or including redundancy in a process
6. Time when equipment or people can't begin working until a specific process completes

Answer:

Transportation is the movement of products or components.

Motion refers to the movement of employees while creating a product or service.

Overproduction is the creation of more products, components, or features than are needed at a particular time.

Inventory is material or information that is not currently needed to create a product or service. This can include material created through overproduction.

Overprocessing is the use of overly large or complex equipment or the inclusion of unnecessary work in a process.

Waiting occurs when equipment or employees have to wait for a previous process to be completed before they can begin working.

ELIMINATING OVERPRODUCTION AND INVENTORY

Eliminating overproduction and inventory

Of all the waste types, Taiichi Ohno viewed overproduction as the worst. This is partly because it tends to result in other forms of waste. In particular, it leads to excess inventory. You produce too much, with the result that you have excess stock, components, or even information to store.

Overproduction and excess inventory can have similar causes. They can result from systems that rely on push production, and from what's known as the just-in-case – or JIC – approach. They can also result from a focus on large batch processing and from poor communication.

Push production

In a push system, material is "pushed" into the production line. As soon as one process completes, its output is passed on to the next stage – irrespective of whether there's enough capacity at that next stage to process the output. The volume of items produced is scheduled ahead of time, usually based on forecasts of customer demand.

Overproduction occurs if demand is overestimated. The excess items produced then accumulate as inventory. Also, excess inventory is common along the production line because of downstream bottlenecks, with more material pushed through the process than it is capable of handling.

JIC

JIC manufacturing refers to overproducing or keeping a large volume of inventory just in case production or supply problems occur. For example, a manufacturer may intentionally overproduce an item if it's known that a certain percentage of the items is likely to be defective. Similarly, a manufacturer who knows that customer demand has a seasonal element may choose to keep a large inventory of products to prevent stock out risks.

Batch processing

Manufacturers may be accustomed to producing large batches of items, leading to overproduction if there isn't immediate demand for all the items. Also, high costs and the time associated with setting up or changing over a production process can mean that it isn't economically viable to produce only a small batch of items.

Poor communication

Poor communication among facilities or stages in the production process can mean that downstream bottlenecks are ignored and that production outstrips demand. Poor communication with suppliers, or an unreliable supply chain, can also result in excess production.

So what can you do to eliminate overproduction and excess inventory? To do this, you can switch to a pull production system, implement poka yoke and other control measures to address the problems that lead to JIC thinking, reduce batch sizes, and improve communication.

Switch to pull production

Changing from a push production system to a pull system helps ensure that you purchase only what the customer or next process requires.

Implement poka yoke

JIC thinking is often tied to potential defects. So you can reduce the waste of overproduction and excess inventory by installing poka yoke – or "mistake-proofing" mechanisms – and by better understanding your equipment's capacity. One example of poka yoke is to use statistical process control, commonly known as SPC, to monitor production outputs and provide early warnings of production problems.

Reduce batch sizes

You can reduce or eliminate batch production by redesigning workflows into single piece flow production. This solution generates an entire product or component, removing the need for batches of components. Other methods could include keeping batch sizes at the level sales demand. Reducing setup and changeover times helps you to produce smaller batches more economically.

Improve communication

If you ensure communication flow between facilities and suppliers, you're better able to shift to a truly pull system, in which each component or item is supplied only when it's needed. This reduces overproduction and the creation of excess inventory.

Say a toy manufacturer receives an order for 1,000 plastic dolls.

The company's plastic molding equipment is time consuming to set up for the required job. Also, it's estimated that up to 5% of the dolls produced will have defects. Accordingly, the manufacturer decides to produce a batch of 3,000 units and assumes that it will be able to sell the left-over dolls to another retailer.

The manufacturer also buys plastic dies and doll hair in bulk – enough for about 3,500 dolls – because the supplier offers a discount.

Question

In which ways could the toy manufacturer reduce waste?

Options:

1. Implement poka yoke to prevent defects
2. Produce only the number of dolls ordered
3. Negotiate favorable terms for smaller orders from suppliers
4. Produce 3,500 dolls to use up all the materials ordered from suppliers
5. Increase the unit price of the dolls

Answer:

Option 1: This option is correct. To make it unnecessary to overproduce or to store the excess units, the manufacturer can install poka yoke to prevent defects from occurring. For example, this might involve installing sensors to ensure the correct plastic molding temperatures and to ensure the correct quantities of die are used.

Option 2: This is a correct option. The manufacturer can prevent overproduction and excess inventory by switching to a pull system, in which only the items for which there's demand are produced. The manufacturer may also be able to shorten setup and changeover times to make creating smaller batches of dolls more economical.

Option 3: This is a correct option. Ordering materials in bulk leads to waste in the form of inventory. Making smaller orders may free up storage space, reduce stock damage, and prevent the need for expensive storage equipment such as forklifts.

Option 4: This is an incorrect option. Any dolls produced over the number actually ordered represent waste.

Option 5: This option is incorrect. It's unlikely the manufacturer could increase the sales price of the dolls after the order has been placed. Also, overproducing and storing inventory constitute waste, irrespective of whether a profit is secured for the items produced.

Next consider an example in the service industry. In a company that creates custom software, developers often create software features that customers haven't specifically requested. Also, company processes require that staff print three copies of any invoice – one to be posted, one to be filed, and one for accounts. These are both examples of overproduction. The copied invoices also represent waste in the form of inventory, because they have to be filed and stored.

To reduce waste, the software company can improve communication between customers and developers, and ensure that developers work only on features customers specifically require. The company could implement an electronic and streamlined invoicing process, keeping it paper free and providing access to invoices via a customer database. And to prevent errors in the invoices or in their storage, the company may install software poka yoke to ensure data is captured correctly and servers are adequately maintained.

MOTION, WAITING, AND TRANSPORTATION

Motion, waiting, and transportation

Excess motion, waiting, and transportation are common in most industries. These types of wastes have similar root causes, including poor design, poor layout, and inadequate training.

Poor design

Poor process design based on push production creates large batch sizes and may result insupply shortages and an unreliable supply chain. And this generates waiting waste. The excess inventory causes transportation waste. If processes aren't carefully designed and workloads balanced, employees need to wait for others to finish – or wait for too many handoffs or approvals – before being able to continue work. Complex material flows, or the sharing of equipment, may also generate the need for transportation and unnecessary movement to collect inventory or equipment.

Poor layout

A lack of defined and standardized work processes results in disorganized work area layouts. In turn, these result in high levels of motion, transportation, and waiting. Messy work areas can result in waiting while an employee finds the right tool or piece of information, and result in unnecessary motion.

Inadequate training

If employees know how to do only one thing and are not cross-trained, they can't be very effective in single-piece production. This results in employees moving from station to station, or excess component transport. Inadequate training and lack of cross-training may also result in inefficient use of equipment and waiting because operators don't know how to maintain or fix equipment problems. Resulting downtime also adds to the waiting waste.

To eliminate motion, transport, and waiting waste based on these core problems, you can apply a mix of solutions. These include good housekeeping, improved layout, standardized work, cross-training, and a variety of strategies for redesigning work processes to reduce batches and bottlenecks.

A ship-building company finds that many of its employees are forced to walk fairly long distances to fetch various tools and components. The company also finds that employees spend considerable amounts of time waiting for components to be finished before assembling them. Finally, the company is spending a large amount of money on forklifts and cranes to transport finished components for assembly.

To address these wastes, a team carefully maps work flows and then assembles all equipment used for one component in a single area. Each area is arranged in a U-shape to minimize the required motion and transportation. To reduce waiting times, the team balances workloads and redesigns the production process to ensure all employees can work in parallel. The team also reduces the distance between workstations.

The company then cross-trains workers so they can use all equipment and perform basic maintenance tasks on it. This reduces the need to move machinery, and employees don't need to walk far to complete their tasks. Training also incorporates best practices for completing assigned tasks efficiently.

Once the work design's improved, the company initiates 5S to create a more ergonomic working area. Unnecessary tools and equipment are removed and tools are placed within easy reach of workers.

The company then initiates a kaizen – or continuous improvement – system to improve the redesigned jobs, which eliminates unnecessary movement and transportation. Best practices, for specific tasks arising from the kaizen event, are standardized and visual aids are used to guide workers in their tasks.

Question

A legal consulting firm notices that its employees waste time searching for documents on messy desks and filing rooms. Hard-copy case files are transported in trolleys from room to room.

In which ways can the firm reduce or eliminate waste?

Options:

1. Organize desks and filing systems using 5S to reduce excess motion

2. Set up a centralized electronic database accessible to all to minimize transportation of paper

3. Set up teams working in parallel on different aspects of a single case to minimize waiting

4. Ensure better communication flow by having teams meet daily for updates to reduce overproduction

5. Create software-based poka yoke to ensure reports contain all required information to prevent defects

Answer:

Option 1: This option is correct. Employees are clearly using excess motion. With neat, user-friendly working spaces, most things should be within reach. This should also reduce waiting times while employees try to locate documents or information.

Option 2: This is a correct option. Moving paper around within service industries is an example of transportation waste. Using electronic data reduces this waste and reduces excess motion. In turn, this should reduce waiting times while employees try to locate documents or information.

Option 3: This option is correct. If teams work in parallel on different aspects of a case, they're less likely to be held up while waiting for information.

Option 4: This option is incorrect. This strategy may be useful if overproduction is occurring due to duplicated research or other work. However, this type of waste isn't apparent in the scenario.

Option 5: This is an incorrect option. Defects don't appear to be a problem in the scenario.

ELIMINATING OVERPROCESSING AND DEFECTS

Eliminating overprocessing and defects

You should now have a sense of how to eliminate five of the seven wastes. But what about overprocessing and defects? Common causes of these two types of waste include poor training, nonstandard work procedures, and poor communication. These can all result in unnecessary or duplicated effort and errors.

Various additional factors can contribute to overprocessing:
- a lack of trust between team members and departments, which can result in too many handoffs, checks, or edits
- incorrect equipment or software, leading to the use of complex workarounds,
- misunderstandings about customer requirements, equipment or supplier capacity, or about a process itself, and
- a lack of innovation, which may leave you with outdated standards that are overly complex

Poor processes, process variation, and inaccurate design, engineering, or machines can cause defects. A lack of skill and insufficient on-the-job support for employees – for example, through mentoring, visual work instructions, and other work guides – can also contribute to defects.

Installing poke yoke and improving training can help to limit both overprocessing and defects. You can also use techniques such as the 5 Whys, statistical process control – also known as SPC, and standard work and procedures. You can further limit overprocessing through kaizen events.

Poka yoke

For example, poka yoke may take the form of equipment sensors or software checks. These automatically reduce defects. They also enable employees to trust in the quality of a product or service. As such, they reduce overprocessing in the form of multiple edits or inspections.

Training

When employees know what to do, they're less likely to make mistakes. Similarly, better understanding of processes and equipment capacity reduces overprocessing. A well-designed and focused training can help achieve these goals.

5 Whys

By asking "why" five times whenever a problem occurs, you're able to find the root causes of defects and overprocessing.

For example, a series of questions and answers may unfold as follows – Why did this customer file a complaint? Because an error appeared in his web site content. Why was there an error? Because the programmer inserted text that was inaccurate. Why did she do that? Because that's how it was sent to her. Why didn't someone check it for accuracy before sending it to her? Because that's not part of the process. Why not? Because until now, proofreading hasn't been necessary.

SPC

SPC involves analyzing variations within a process. Variations cause errors, so minimizing variation reduces errors. For example, an assembly process produced goods with a high proportion of defects. It was believed that the defects were a result of excessive variation. SPC was applied to monitor and analyze variation in the assembly process. Analysis revealed that the variation was caused by inaccurate manual measurement of the base unit. The team then installed an electronic measurement device that helped reduce variation and defects significantly in the process.

Standard work

Like SPC, standard work minimizes variations and so reduces errors. It ensures a task is completed the same way each time. If operators always use exactly four turns to tighten a screw, for example, there will be fewer loose screws.

Kaizen events

A kaizen event is a brief and structured improvement initiative. A cross-functional team is tasked with gathering baseline data, identifying waste, and finding and implementing solutions.

The event helps to shift employees and managers to a continuous improvement mindset. This can help them to recognize and avoid overprocessing. For example, it may lead to a recognition that having five managers sign off on a component or service is unnecessary.

Through careful observation, you'll be able to identify types of waste within your organization. Recognizing these and using strategies to reduce them can streamline your business and boost the bottom line.

Question

A detergent manufacturer notices that its chemical testing processes are cumbersome and take too long. Also, a great deal of rework is required, which is noted at the final quality check. It also observes that a high number of product bottles are overfilled as they move along the conveyor belt.

In which ways can the manufacturer reduce or eliminate waste?

Options:

1. Add speed sensor to the conveyor belt to ensure speed does not vary when bottling the detergent

2. Initiate a kaizen event to streamline the chemical testing process

3. Use the 5 Whys technique to determine the cause of transportation waste between bottling and deliveries

4. Incorporate brief quality checks by operators at the start and end of each task to prevent defects

5. Ensure better communication flow by having testing and production employees meet daily to reduce overproduction

Answer:

Option 1: This option is correct. Installing poka yoke such as the sensor will reduce waste in the form of defects.

Option 2: This is a correct option. It's likely that overprocessing is occurring in the cumbersome chemical testing processes. A kaizen event should help to eliminate this form of waste.

Option 3: This option is incorrect. Transportation waste isn't mentioned in this scenario. Also, transporting products to the customer isn't considered to be waste.

Option 4: This option is correct. Instead of waiting for the final quality check, checks at each phase of the process should dramatically reduce errors and therefore the need for later rework.

Option 5: This is an incorrect option. Overproduction waste isn't mentioned in the scenario.

SECTION 3 - CONTINUOUS FLOW AND LINE BALANCING

SECTION 3 - Continuous Flow and Line Balancing

Removing obstacles and bottlenecks helps you to achieve continuous flow – ensuring customers receive the right work, in the correct quantity, at the right time.

Line balancing is the primary Lean tool for achieving continuous flow. To balance a line, you need to calculate cycle times, calculate takt time, and create an operator balance chart. Using this information, you can determine the optimum number of operators per process and then spread work evenly among them so that each task is completed within its takt time.

CONTINUOUS FLOW

Continuous flow

Imagine a production process that's free of interruptions, delays, and backlogs, right from the supply of raw materials to the distribution of goods or services. This ideal process represents the concept of continuous flow.

When you achieve continuous flow, you ensure employees and external customers receive the right work, in the correct quantity, at the right time. Creating continuous flow decreases production costs because it aims to cut queue times and work-in- process inventory. It involves cross-training workers and this results in greater flexibility. It also involves standardizing work, which results in fewer errors. This in turn reduces frustration and waiting times. Good flow also helps employees identify errors early in a process.

An automobile manufacturer desperately needs to decrease production times, reduce rework because of errors, and cut costs. To do this, it first maps its production flow and, using Lean techniques, begins the process of creating continuous flow. By reducing batch sizes, using kanban, and switching from a push to a pull production system, the manufacturer dramatically reduces queues and in-process inventory.

It negotiates with suppliers for more frequent and smaller deliveries, and streamlines the shipping of vehicles to its customers. The result? Production times are halved and the company saves millions of dollars.

Question

What are the benefits of achieving the goals of continuous flow in your operations?

Options:

1. Decreased production time
2. Greater flexibility
3. Fewer errors and earlier error detection
4. Increased rate of production
5. Greater specialization of employees

Answer:

Option 1: This option is correct. Improving flow involves removing obstacles and delays, and so decreases production time.

Option 2: This is a correct option. Because employees are cross trained, they are more capable of changing their practices to meet changes in customer demand.

Option 3: This option is correct. Through the use of standard work, fewer errors are made and problems are noticed earlier.

Option 4: This option is incorrect. The aim of achieving continuous flow isn't necessarily to increase the rate of production. In a pull production system, you create only as much as the customer requires.

Option 5: This is an incorrect option. Achieving continuous flow typically involves cross-training workers, rather than increasing their levels of specialization. Cross-training provides benefits such as greater flexibility.

LINE BALANCING

Line balancing

The Lean method for achieving continuous flow is known as line balancing. This involves organizing your production line and employees so that work is balanced evenly according to task and each person spends the same amount of time on a task. This balancing process optimizes flow because it eliminates wait times between the steps in a process.

In an example of an unbalanced production line, operator A takes just over 2 minutes to complete her task. Operator B takes almost 5 minutes to complete his task. So inventory will build up before operator B can work on it. Also, operator C has to wait for him to finish before she can complete her 2-minute task.

To balance the line, operators A and C are each given 1 minute of extra work, which is taken from the work of operator B. As a result, all the operators take 3 minutes per task.

In some cases, the last person in a process is given slightly less work, to account for the extra time it takes to move a component on to the next process. However, common sense and careful judgment is always the highest priority. So when allocating work that can't be divided evenly, operators should guide you to determine what would be best.

Question

Consider an unbalanced production line. It takes operator A 10 minutes to complete a task. Operator B needs 35 minutes per task, and operator C takes 15 minutes per task.

How would you reorganize the work to balance the production line?

Options:

1. Move 10 minutes worth of work from operator B to operator A, and move 5 minutes worth of work from operator B to operator C

2. Move 5 minutes worth of work from operator B to operator A and to operator C

3. Move 10 minutes worth of work from operator B to operator C and to operator A

Answer:

Option 1: This option is correct. To balance the line, you need to ensure each operator requires the same amount of time to complete a task – in this case 20 minutes.

Option 2: This option is incorrect. If you did this, operator A would have 15 minutes work per task, operator B would have 25 minutes work, and operator C would have 20 minutes work. The line would still be unbalanced.

Option 3: This option is incorrect. If you did this, operator A would have 20 minutes work per task, operator B would have 15 minutes work, and operator C would have 25 minutes work. The line would still be unbalanced.

CYCLE AND TAKT TIMES

Cycle and takt times

To implement line balancing, you use a five-step process. First you calculate the cycle time and then takt time. Using this information, you create an operator balance chart, and then you determine the ideal number of operators. Finally, you balance the work using the information you've gathered.

Cycle time is the time it takes an operator to complete a task and move a product or component to the next operator in line. Before calculating cycle time, you should explain to operators what you'll be doing and why. Then you observe and time their actions. Suppose you're balancing the final process for manufacturing a precision tool. This process has three steps – operators attach a lever, inspect the tool, and pack it. Once these steps are complete, the tool is handed over for shipping.

To capture the timing data, you use a cycle time worksheet. You enter operator names in the Operator column and task descriptions in the Task column. In this example, the operators are named A, B, and C, and the tasks are Attach lever, Inspect, and Pack.

Typically, you should use a video camera with a timer to record what each operator does. Then you enter the observed times in the Sample times columns. The norm is to record 10 sample times per task though the example here, showing six samples, is simplified for the training purpose.

From the sample times, you then extract key data, including the most frequent time observed, the highest time, and the lowest repeatable time.

Most frequent

The most frequent time is used as a baseline from which you can work to improve the time to low repeatable if possible. This time is used to calculate the total cycle time for the three tasks in the process.

High

You use the High time to isolate potentially recurring problems in the process so that you can work on preventing them in the future. If a problem isn't addressed, it's likely to disrupt flow and may even cause the process to fail.

Low repeat

You can use the low repeatable figures to set realistic target times for each task. Find out what operators did or what occurred in the environment to allow these times. Then attempt to standardize this so that low repeats become the most frequent times.

It's important you don't count a single occurrence of a low time as repeatable because this is likely to be an unreasonable target time.

You calculate the total cycle time for the process by adding the most frequent time for each task. In this case, you add 3, 2, and 2.6 minutes to get a total of 7.6 minutes.

In the example, just one operator is assigned to each task. Realistically, you could have multiple operators performing the same work simultaneously or a single operator performing multiple tasks. Your cycle time worksheet should be designed to reflect your actual production processes.

Once you've worked out the cycle times for a process, you need to calculate the takt time. This is a measure of how fast operators must work to produce products at a pace that's perfectly in tune with customer demand. You calculate takt time by dividing net available time per period by customer demand per period.

Say each shift lasts eight hours, or 480 minutes. Customer demand equates to 120 products per shift. So to find takt time, you divide 480 by 120. This gives you 4 minutes per unit product. In practice though, remember you need to adjust the net operating time to include time operators spend on breaks, meetings, and other activities.

OPERATOR AND WORK BALANCE

Operator and work balance

Once you've calculated the cycle time and takt time for a process, you move on to the third step – creating an operator balance chart. This chart depicts the current state of work.

In an operator balance chart, the cycle times are shown on the vertical axis. In this scenario, they're measured in minutes. The horizontal axis lists the operators. Each bar in the bar chart shows an operator's most frequent time for completing a task. A line depicting takt time cuts across the 4-minute mark.

The chart shows that the tasks are unbalanced and that overproduction is occurring, because all tasks are completed in less time than the takt time. After you've created an operator balance chart, you need to determine the ideal number of operators. The formula for doing this is the total cycle time divided by takt time. For example, if your total cycle time is 160 minutes and the takt time is 30 minutes, the ideal number of operators would be 5.3.

Question

If the takt time for a process is 4 minutes and the total cycle time is 7.6 minutes, what is the ideal number of operators for the process?

Use up to two decimal places in your answer if necessary.

Operator A has a cycle time of 3 minutes, operator B has a cycle time of 2 minutes, and operator C has a cycle time of 2.6 minutes. A dotted horizontal line representing takt time is positioned at the 4-minute mark in the bar chart.

Answer:

You divide the total cycle time, 7.6, by the takt time, 4.

The result for the calculation is 1.9. So ideally, you need only two operators – rather than three – for the process. You use this information to complete the final step – balancing the work. In this step, you use the ideal number of operators, ensuring they require the same amount of time per task and they perform to takt time, no faster and no slower.

Because the ideal number of operators is two, your balanced chart will have only two bars. The two need to complete their tasks within the 4-minute takt time. So the work needs to be divided as evenly as possible between operators A and B.

Some of operator B's inspection work should fall to operator A to bring her up to takt time. In this case, assigning her 1 minute of inspection work brings her per-task completion time to 4 minutes.

A 1-minute check and the packing task should fall to operator B, bringing her total cycle time to 3.6 minutes. Typically, if the figures aren't perfect, it's best to give the final worker in the process slightly less work than indicated by takt time, to allow extra time for moving the product to the next process.

If your calculation for the ideal number of operators works out at 3.5 operators, you can't employ half a person. In this instance, you would need four operators. You can arrange this so the first three work to takt time. The fourth works half time to perform the final task and spends the rest of a shift on a different process if possible.

It's not always possible to divide labor in a way that lets you achieve perfect takt time. You need to use good judgment about how best to distribute work so that everyone works as close to takt time as possible, and no worker is overloaded.

As in manufacturing contexts, you can use line balancing in service environments to ensure the optimal number of people work at the optimal pace and to help achieve continuous flow. Typically, you focus on balancing the work associated with an individual service offering or a specific administrative function.

In the shipping industry, packing materials into delivery vehicles such as trucks or boats is a service offering that could benefit from line balancing. In IT departments, maintenance work on employees' PCs is an IT service that could be optimized through line balancing.

Similarly, mechanics can optimize standard tasks such as removing engines using this method.

Case Study: Question 1 of 4
Scenario

In a large financial institution, three back-office analysts prepare batch jobs of financials for separate branches across the world. The analysts work from 7:00 p.m. to 12:30 a.m. with a half-hour break during that period – so they each work for 300 minutes per day. In this time, analysts are expected to complete 60 batches of work.

The analysts have been complaining they never finish on time, despite some of them having to wait around. You've been brought in to balance the line. Answer the questions in the given order.

Question

The first analyst gathers data, the second codes the data, and the third encrypts and sends the data. You begin by capturing cycle time data on a worksheet.

Which times should you record?

Options:

1. The longest time it takes each analyst to finish a task

2. The shortest time any analyst takes with a task

3. The most frequent time that it takes for each analyst to complete a task

4. The shortest repeatable time it takes each analyst to complete a task

5. Cycle times that are closest to takt time

Answer:

Option 1: This option is correct. By finding out what causes spikes in the workload, you can find root problems in the flow and prevent them from occurring.

Option 2: This option is incorrect. Because this time is not repeated, it doesn't represent a reasonable target time for tasks.

Option 3: This is a correct option. The most frequent time taken to complete a task is used as a baseline measure. It is used to calculate the optimum number of operators per process.

Option 4: This option is correct. If short times are repeated, it may be possible to standardize practices that result in shorter cycle times.

Option 5: This is an incorrect option. You goal is to calculate cycle time. The next step in line balancing is to calculate takt time.

Case Study: Question 2 of 4

Customer demand is 60 batches of work from each 300 minute shift.

What is the takt time for the process?

Options:

1. 5 minutes
2. 20 seconds
3. 5.5 minutes
4. 2 minutes

Answer:

Option 1: This is the correct option. To calculate takt time, you divide the net number of minutes – in this case 300 – by the customer requirements per period – 60. This results in a 5-minute takt time.

Option 2: This option is incorrect. Here you have divided 60 by 300. To calculate takt time, you divide the net number of minutes – in this case 300 – by the customer requirements per period – 60.

Option 3: This is an incorrect option. You don't add the 30 minute break that the analysts take. So the takt time is 300 divided by 60, which equals 5.

Option 4: This option is incorrect. To calculate takt time, you divide the net number of minutes – in this case 300 – by the customer requirements per period – 60. This results in a 5-minute takt time.

Case Study: Question 3 of 4

Given the cycle time totals and a takt time of 5 minutes, what is the ideal number of analysts for this process?

In a cycle time worksheet for the process, the most frequent times for completing the three relevant tasks are 7, 8, and 5 minutes respectively. This gives a total of 20 minutes. The highest recorded times for completing the three tasks are 9, 9.5, and 6 minutes – giving a total of 24.5 minutes. The low repeat times for the tasks are 6, 7, and 4.5 minutes, giving a total of 17.5 minutes.

Options:
1. Four
2. Three
3. Two
4. Five

Answer:

Option 1: This is the correct option. To determine the optimum number of analysts, you divide the total for the most frequent cycle times – 20 – by the takt time – 5. So four analysts would be ideal.

Option 2: This option is incorrect. To determine the optimum number of analysts, you need to divide the total for the most frequent cycle times – 20 – by the takt time – 5.

Option 3: This is an incorrect option. You divide the total for the most frequent cycle times – 20 – by the takt time – 5 to determine the optimum number of analysts for a process.

Option 4: This option is incorrect. You divide the total for the most frequent cycle times – 20 – by the takt time – 5 to determine the optimum number of analysts for a process.

Case Study: Question 4 of 4

In which way could you balance the line for the process?

The current state operator balance chart shows three operators. Operator A's cycle time is 7 minutes, operator B's cycle time is 8 minutes, and operator C's cycle time is 5 minutes. Takt time is given as 5 minutes.

Options:

1. Add a new analyst – operator D – and assign this person two minutes of gathering work from operator A and three minutes of coding work from operator B

2. Redistribute work so that operators A and B complete their tasks within 7.5 minutes, and operator C completes a task within 5 minutes

3. Add a new analyst and redistribute the work so that operator A spends 7 minutes per data gathering task, both operators B and C take 4 minutes per coding task, and operator D spends 5 minutes per task

Answer:

Option 1: This is the correct option. Redistributing the work in this way will result in each of the four analysts – which is the ideal number of operators – spending five minutes of work per batch. This ensures the analysts' task cycle times match takt time. The work will be evenly distributed.

Option 2: This option is incorrect. Although you've balanced the workload of operators A and B, both are working over takt time. Also, operator C will spend time waiting for the others to complete their tasks.

Option 3: This is an incorrect option. Although you've balanced the coding work, both coders are working below takt time and operator A has too much work to do.

CHAPTER V - VALUE STREAM MAPPING IN LEAN BUSINESS

CHAPTER V - Value Stream Mapping in Lean Business
   SECTION 1 - Introduction to Value Stream Mapping
   SECTION 2 - Mapping the Current State
   SECTION 3 - Mapping the Future State

VALUE STREAM MAPPING

Value stream mapping

A value stream describes the flow of materials and information that bring a product or service to a customer. In other words, it's the way that value is delivered – from the source, or starting point – right through to delivery to the customer. Any obstacles or waste, such as wasted time, unnecessary motion, or excess inventory, will disrupt the flow of value in a value stream.

You need a clear picture of a full value stream before you can determine where waste is occurring or plan how the flow of value to the customer can be made more efficient. A useful tool for obtaining this picture is a value stream map. This type of map graphically represents the flow of material and information through various production activities.

It also depicts the flow of steps in product management-and-information systems that support these activities.

When analyzing a value stream for inefficiencies, you need to create two maps. The first map reflects the current state of a process or system, while the second map reflects its future state.

Current state

A current-state value stream map is a visual representation of a process as it currently stands. This map provides a starting point for identifying waste and its causes.

Future state

A future-state value stream map represents the targeted state of the process, or its state once improvements have been implemented. The map highlights areas in the process where improvement initiatives are required and what flows should be altered to create a leaner production and information flow.

Creating a current-state value stream map involves measuring, documenting, and analyzing complex relationships between process steps. Doing this provides insight into both decision-making and physical processes. This insight equips you to plan improvements to operations and organizational structure. You then represent these improvements in a future-state value stream map, which depicts the goals for improvement initiatives.

Value stream mapping is a five-step process. First you identify a product or service for which you want to create a map. Then you create a current-state map of the value stream for that product or service. You follow this by assessing the current value stream, identifying waste and opportunities for improvement. Then you create a future-state map. Finally, you develop and implement a plan to bring the value stream closer to the future state you've depicted.

Question
What are the key objectives of value stream mapping?

Options:
1. To provide a "big-picture" overview of a value stream
2. To gain insight into decision-making and physical processes
3. To help you identify waste and opportunities for improvement
4. To help you plan improvements to operations and organizational structure
5. To link all products in a product family
6. To implement pull rather than push systems

Answer:
Option 1: This option is correct. A value stream map provides a visual representation of an entire value stream, including both material and information flows. So it provides an overview of the value stream and the complex relationships within it.

Option 2: This is a correct option. Because you have to measure, document, and analyze complex relationships to create a current-state value stream map, you gain insight into decision-making and physical processes.

Option 3: This option is correct. A value stream map graphically represents an entire value stream. This makes it easier to identify instances of waste and opportunities for improvements.

Option 4: This is a correct option. A future-state value stream map helps set improvement targets, guiding efforts to improve current operations and decision-making.

Option 5: This is an incorrect option. The main purpose of value stream mapping is to aid in understanding and analyzing a value stream so that improvements can be made to it.

Option 6: This option is incorrect. The types of changes needed to improve efficiency and optimize the flow of value in an organization will depend on issues within the mapped value stream.

CREATING A CURRENT-STATE MAP

Creating a current-state map

The first step in value stream mapping is deciding exactly what to map. You need to identify which product or service will benefit most from more efficient processes. You also need to decide on the scope of the map. For example, what must its beginning and end points be? And should you focus on improving the full value stream or only a specific process?

The answers should depend on the specific problems or inefficiencies it's important for your organization to address. For example, high overall production costs may indicate that part of the value stream dealing with production processes needs review. A drop in sales may mean that only your organization's sales process, or perhaps the parts of the value stream related to product quality, should be mapped.

To help you decide what product or service to map, you might consider which has the highest number of defects, which has the highest product volume in either dollars or units, or which has links to the most processes.

You might also choose a product or service based on factors specific to its customer or its destination. For example, you might focus on a service that a high-profile client uses or on a product for distribution in a particular region.

In general, value stream mapping is appropriate for routine or standardized processes.

It isn't likely to pay off if your business continually changes its work processes or products – for example with completely new processes for each project it undertakes. Value stream mapping can be useful in both manufacturing and service environments. The type of environment you're in will help determine what to map.

Manufacturing

In manufacturing, it works to map static activities or tasks – such as welding security doors, or creating and bottling soda. Here, the tasks have relatively low labor content and very few alternative flows exist.

Service

In service industries, you work with four basic flows – people, processes, technology, and time. Creating value stream maps based on these flows can help you identify interactions and management controls. It can also help identify how changes to one of the flows will impact the other three.

Many flows in an office environment begin with a paper or e-mail request. Following progress from receipt of this request typically takes you through the activities required for a specific service.

An example can help to illustrate the type of service you might identify for a value stream map. A Human Resources Department wants to map the processing of job applications. Activities in the process include screening resumes, scheduling interviews, conducting interviews, and making hiring decisions. In this process flow, each activity either adds or fails to add value to the final product – which in this case is the recruitment of a candidate.

Once you've identified the product or service you want to map, you create a current-state map of the value stream. This map shows work processes as they currently exist. As well as making it possible to identify improvement opportunities, the map serves as a baseline measure against which you can compare future results.

To create a current-state map, you need to gather data, walking backward through the relevant process – from delivery to the customer to the beginning of the process.

Elements that you'll capture in the map include data related to cycle times, people involved in the process, as well as process, material, and information flows.

A current-state map typically uses specific icons to represent each type of data:
- a square or rectangle represents a physical process,
- a triangle labeled with an "I" represents inventory,
- a straight, striped arrow or sometimes a solid arrow signifies an item being pushed to a subsequent step, and a curved arrow represents an item being physically pulled to that step,
- a circle with a semi-circle below it identifies an operator,
- a zigzag arrow represents electronic information flow, a narrow straight arrow is for face-to-face

communication, and paper communication is shown as a labeled rectangle – for example labeled "Weekly fax",
- an image of a ship, truck, or plane represents transport, and
- a building icon – consisting of a box topped by a zigzag – represents a supplier, distributor, or customer.

This map illustrates four processes in a material flow between a supplier and a distributor. Materials are transported from the supplier once a day, are subject to four processes, and are transported to a distributor once a month.

Straight, striped arrows indicate that materials are pushed from one process to the next, and each process has an inventory triangle. The top of the map uses zigzag arrows – which represent electronic communication – to show that production control receives quarterly forecasts from the distributor and sends weekly faxes to the supplier.

Question

Which icon represents inventory?

Options:

1. A triangle
2. A truck
3. A circle with a semi-circle below it
4. A square

Answer:

Option 1: This is the correct option. A triangle – often labeled with an "I" – represents inventory in a value stream map.

Option 2: This option is incorrect. A truck represents transport in a value stream map.

Option 3: This is an incorrect option. A circle with a semi-circle below it represents an operator in a value stream map.

Option 4: This option is incorrect. A square represents a process in a value stream map.

CREATING AND USING A FUTURE-STATE MAP

Creating and using a future-state map

Once you've created a current-state value stream map, you assess it to identify sources of waste. Examples are wasted time, unnecessary effort and motion, excess inventory, unnecessary transport of goods, or a procedure performed by too many people. Other common waste areas to target include unnecessary use of equipment, inefficient quality checks, stockpiling of finished products, and the addition of features that the customer doesn't value.

In this value stream map, inventory is a potential area of waste for each process. Also, each process is activated by push material flow, which builds work-in-process inventory unnecessarily. A possible cause of this waste is too little communication between production control and both the supplier and distributor. Once you've identified problems with the current flow, you move on to step four – creating a future-state map. This map is intended to eliminate sources of waste and to balance the production line to meet customer demand.

Eliminate sources of waste

As with any Lean project, eliminating waste is key. Any type of waste is likely to slow processes and cost money, while adding nothing of value to the customer. Although you can't fix everything at once, you need to identify key waste areas and remove them from the future-state map. Once this improved state is reached, you can use the future-state map as a current-state map and repeat the process.

Balance production line

Balancing the production line helps ensure you don't exceed customer demand by overproducing, or that you don't fall short of customer demand by creating defects or missing deadlines for delivery. You can't make everything perfect at the first attempt. You start with serious bottlenecks or high internal inventory areas. Once the targeted future state is reached, you can continue to improve the production line by moving through the value stream mapping process again.

The future-state map provides a strategic plan for improving a value stream. It creates a visual overview of what you'd like a process to be in a few months time. Teams can use the map to focus tactical changes.

The final step in value stream mapping is to develop and implement a plan to achieve the future state you've mapped. Typically, areas for improvement are broadly highlighted on the future-state map, with kaizen stars used to indicate areas identified for improvement. When developing the plan, you use the value stream map to highlight the goals and objectives for the team. The team should include those working with the relevant processes to ensure buy-in.

This team works out the details of how to make the improvements outlined in the future-state map. Rewarding efficient work and improvement suggestions can also help stimulate improvements. The plan highlights the types of interventions needed. For example, these might be "just-do-it" fixes that can be implemented in a day, kaizen blitzes that take two to five days, or longer-term projects. These are generally structured as aspects of a kaizen event.

Question

Sequence the steps in the value stream mapping process in the correct order.

Options:

A. Identify the product
B. Map the current state
C. Assess the current state
D. Map the future state
E. Implement the action plan

Answer:

Identify the product is ranked the first step. Identifying the product or service you intend to map is the first step in the process.

Map the current state is ranked the second step. Creating a current-state map to provide an overview of the current process is the second step of the process.

Assess the current state is ranked the third step. Assessing the current-state map for waste and opportunities for improvement is the third step in the process.

Map the future state is ranked the fourth step. Creating a future-state map as a goal and guide for improvements is the fourth step in the process.

Implement the action plan is ranked the fifth step. Implementing an action plan to achieve the future state you've mapped is the final step in the process.

A pharmaceutical manufacturing company decides to use value stream mapping for a top-selling generic pain relief tablet. A process improvement team maps the production of the tablet, from receiving supplies to delivery to the distributor. Developing a current-state map allows everyone on the team to access the entire process. Team members will understand how their way of working impacts each process along the line. They're also able to contextualize the process with a focus on the customer's needs.

The team members review the map, discussing obvious signs of wastes. They select inventory and changeover times for improvement and create a future-state map to represent the improvements. Within three months, the team is able to reduce inventory by 25% and production time by 15%.

Question

Which do you think are the benefits of value stream mapping for the team?

Options:

1. Helps the team to identify wastes and their sources
2. Creates a shared vision that clarifies where waste is occurring
3. Provides a customer-focused base from which to design kaizen events

4. Allows the team to see the big picture and plan accordingly

5. Provides tactical details of how improvements should be made

6. Focuses on material and information flows

Answer:

Option 1: This is a correct option. Because a value stream map provides an overview of an entire process, it makes it easier to identify where waste is occurring.

Option 2: This option is correct. Because everyone on a team uses a current-state value stream map as their frame of reference, a shared vision of a process is created. This includes a shared understanding of where waste is occurring.

Option 3: This is a correct option. Value stream maps are based on value streams linking processes to customers. This helps to form a customer-focused base from which improvements can be made.

Option 4: This option is correct. Value stream maps provide an overview of an entire process, including all relevant material and information flows.

Option 5: This option is incorrect. A value stream map doesn't document tactical plans. However, a future-state map identifies the target state that tactical plans should achieve.

Option 6: This is an incorrect option. Value stream maps provide an overview of current processes and strategic targets for improvement. They don't necessarily focus on material or information flows.

So value stream maps are useful because they create a common vision of targeted value streams, helping teams to identify waste and its sources. The big-picture view that the maps provide help teams to develop improvement plans based on a customer-focused approach.

SECTION 1 - INTRODUCTION TO VALUE STREAM MAPPING

SECTION 1 - Introduction to Value Stream Mapping

Value stream mapping is a five-step process. First you identify the product or service you want to map, and then you create a current-state map of the identified area. The third step is to assess the current value stream, identifying waste and opportunities for improvement. In step four, you create a future-state map and, in step five, you develop and implement a plan to bring you closer to that future state.

Value stream maps are useful because they create a common vision of targeted value streams, helping teams to identify waste and its sources, and to develop improvement plans based on a customer-focused approach.

SECTION 2 - MAPPING THE CURRENT STATE

SECTION 2 - Mapping the Current State

To map the current state of a value stream, you first gather data, working backward from the last to the first step in the process. Once you've gathered relevant data, you draw the shell of the map, starting with the customer and the supplier. You then add processes, starting with the final process and ending with the first one. After you've added all processes, you flesh the map out using the data you gathered.

GATHERING DATA

Gathering data

You create a current-state value stream map to get a clear overview of a particular process and to gather baseline data so you can plan improvements. Once you have a product, process, or area target, you gather the data, draw the shell of the map, and then flesh out the information it contains.

To gather data, you may need such things as a clipboard with each process listed, a stopwatch, a list of questions that you can use to obtain relevant data, and – in some cases – a video camera.

The data you need to gather includes cycle times, changeover times, uptime, number of operators at each station, inventory amounts, batch sizes, working time, and defect rate. You gather this data on site by observing the operators at work, starting at the final step of the process and working your way back to the first step.

As you observe, you should ask operators questions about the process. They know the process better than anyone. To find out more about information flows, for example, you can ask how they're informed about what to work on next, how often they receive a schedule, how they pass work on once it's completed, and how they access new components to work on.

A kaizen team for an auto parts manufacturer targets the bumper manufacturing process. It begins by gathering data for a current-state value stream map. The team documents the weekly delivery of 2,000 bumpers to the manufacturer's two main customers. It notes that the warehouse has three weeks of stored inventory and that delivery details are e-mailed to customers.

The team then walks back through the inspection, painting, machining, molding, and fabrication processes. For each process, it determines the number of operators, cycle times, inventory numbers, changeover times, and uptimes for equipment.

By speaking to operators, the team discovers that the painting, machining, molding, and fabrication operators all receive a daily schedule from the production manager. The manager communicates this schedule in person.

Question

Now consider a service company. A charity organization receives food donations and distributes these to the local area food banks. The organization wants to streamline the process. It begins by mapping the current value stream.

What types of questions should the team ask operators while gathering information?

Options:
1. How long does it take to pack the delivery truck?
2. How many delivery trucks do you have?
3. How is the driver notified of delivery details?

4. Who informs you when the food items are sorted and are ready to tag?

5. What is the passenger capacity of the trucks?

6. What do you use to tag donations?

Answer:

Option 1: This is a correct option. Time flows are among the key flows in service delivery, so it's useful to ask how long workers need to pack a delivery truck.

Option 2: This option is correct. Process flows are among the key flows in service industries. It's important to find out how many trucks you have to make deliveries. This will provide good baseline data.

Option 3: This is a correct option. Information flows are among the key flows in service industries. It's important to determine how information is delivered.

Option 4: This option is correct. People and communication flows are key flows in service industries, so it's important to determine who does what and when.

Option 5: This option is incorrect. The storage carrying capacity of the trucks is important to flow, not the passenger space.

Option 6: This option is incorrect. What you use to communicate how the products are sorted has little to with the value flow.

CREATING THE MAP

Creating the map

Once you've gathered all the relevant information, you create the shell of a value stream map. You start by adding the customer and supplier at either ends of the map. Next you add the processes, starting with the final step – typically delivering the finished product.

In the auto parts manufacturing example, the team starts with the source symbols. The supplier is placed on the left – the usual starting point for a material flow – and the customer is placed on the right, which is the usual end point for a material flow. Then the team adds two truck symbols to represent delivery by truck and five main processes, which are fabrication, molding, machining, painting, and inspection.

Question

Which current-state value stream map has been started correctly?

Options:

1. The map shows a "Supplier" icon on the left and a "Distributor" icon on the right. A truck icon displays

below the distributor, and below that are three process rectangles.

2. The "Distributor" icon displays above the truck icon. A straight arrow connects the truck icon to "Distributor". Below the truck symbol is the "Manufacturing" process. It is connected to the truck symbol by a straight line.

3. The map shows two processes, labeled "Painting" and "Shipping". Between each process is an inventory triangle.

Answer:

Option 1: This is the correct option. The map starts with the source symbols, which are those of the supplier on the left and the distributor on the right. The truck symbol is added below the source symbols. Finally, three processes are added, typically starting with the last and moving to the first.

Option 2: This option is incorrect. Although the map shows that you're beginning with the customer – the distributor, the supplier has not been added even though details about the processes are already in the map.

Option 3: This is an incorrect option. When creating the map shell, you begin by adding the customer and supplier, and then add process boxes – starting with the last step in the process and moving to the first.

Once you've created the shell, you map the production flow. Follow along as the production flow for the auto parts manufacturer is mapped.

You add truck icons to depict delivery from the supplier to the customer. You connect the processes with push arrows, indicating that material flow is pushed to the next phase once completed.

You add the number of operators and the operator icon for each process to the top of the process boxes. For example, the fabrication process uses three operators and the molding process uses five operators.

You add process data for each process in the data process boxes. These contain details about cycle times, changeover times, and uptimes. For example, the fabrication process has a cycle time of 5 minutes, a changeover time of 45 minutes, and an uptime of 90%.

You place inventory triangles to the left of each process that uses inventory and record the amount of inventory. For example, the inventory icon to the left of the molding process shows that 4,400 items of inventory are passed to it from the fabrication process.

You add information arrows between icons to show the information flow. For example, production planning control sends a weekly schedule to the production manager, who sends a daily schedule to the personnel responsible for each process. The customer sends a quarterly demand to production planning control and production planning control sends a quarterly production plan to the suppliers.

The jagged arrows between processes, supplier sources, and customer sources indicate that aspects of the information flow between these entities are electronic. Putting a lead-time ladder along the bottom of the map is the final step. In the ladder, the peaks represent the lead time between each process.

The troughs represent the value-added time associated with each process. To get the total lead time, the team totals the lead time associated with each process. The total value-added time is the total of the time indicated in the troughs – in this case, 43 minutes.

Question

A current-state value stream map represents a charity's food donation process. What information is missing?

In the map, an arrow connects a rectangle labeled "Donation center" to a truck icon labeled "1 × daily" and then to a rectangle labeled "Empty Truck." This rectangle links to another rectangle labeled "Sort", which in turn links to a rectangle labeled "Inspect & tag." This links to a rectangle labeled "Shipping/Staging." The Shipping/Staging rectangle leads up to a truck icon labeled "1 × daily" and then to a building icon labeled "Local area food bank." The "Empty truck", "Sort", "Inspect & tag", and "Shipping/Staging" rectangles are linked by straight, striped arrows, each of which have a triangle labeled "I" attached to them. The number 2, followed by a circle within a semicircle, appear in the "Empty truck", "Sort", and "Inspect & tag" rectangles.

Options:

1. Data about how much inventory is kept
2. Information flows that trigger and monitor production flows
3. A lead time ladder, showing lead times and value-added times
4. Whether material flows are push or pull
5. The number of operators for each process

Answer:

Option 1: This option is correct. The inventory triangles aren't labeled with actual inventory amounts, so it's not clear how much inventory is kept for each process.

Option 2: This is a correct option. Only the production flow is mapped. Information flow is not shown.

Option 3: This option is correct. The lead time ladder is typically placed beneath the map and provides lead and value-added time data.

Option 4: This is an incorrect option. The striped push arrows between processes show that material flows are pushed rather than pulled in this example.

Option 5: This option is incorrect. The circle with a semi-circle icons depict the number of operators for each process.

SECTION 3 - MAPPING THE FUTURE STATE

SECTION 3 - Mapping the Future State

To create a future-state value stream map, you analyze the current-state map to identify areas of waste. You then determine the root causes for this waste. Next you identify process blocks by identifying process cycle times that exceed takt time.

You can address these bottlenecks using strategies such as line balancing or one-piece flow production design. These strategies work best for predictable and repeatable tasks.

When tasks aren't predictable, it's best to introduce pull flow, using strategies such as post or signal kanbans. With a pull system, flow is pulled by the customer from the final process, and each process pulls from an earlier task.

IDENTIFYING WASTE

Identifying waste

Future-state value stream maps provide strategic direction for improvements and help you to develop performance metrics, for measuring performance and comparing it against the current-state baseline. So they provide measurable goals for process improvements.

To develop a future-state value stream map, you follow a three-step process:
1. identify sources of waste highlighted in the current-state map,
2. identify process blocks – or areas where bottlenecks are occurring, and
3. balance the production line.

The first step is identifying sources of waste by reviewing the current-state map you created. Once you've identified waste, you can use the 5 Whys process to help determine its root cause. This means you ask five "why" questions regarding the waste.

For example, if an operator spends five minutes gathering required components, you ask why. You find that the stock is kept in a separate room in five different boxes. So you ask why again. You repeat this process five or more times until you uncover the source of the problem. Some examples of types of waste you might identify are excess motion, overproduction, excess inventory, and overprocessing.

Excess motion

Excess motion refers to unnecessary movement and walking time on the part of process operators.

For example, assembly line workers may make several trips to collect components for assembling into a home theater system. Placing a stock of components closer to the operators and providing them with a trolley for collecting larger numbers of components at a time could help reduce the wasted motion.

Overproduction

Overproduction occurs when more components or products are created than are needed at a particular time.

For example, an operator produces ten welds a minute. The next operator in the line sands the welds and drills holes for assembly. The stack of welded metal gets higher and higher because the second operator can't keep up the pace set by the first operator. Adding a third operator at the second station, or having the first operator sand the welds, could solve this problem.

Excess inventory

Excess inventory is unnecessary storage of materials, components, or products. A build-up of piles of welded components at a particular point in an assembly line is an example of excess inventory. The components take up space and can't be processed in time. A large bin of bolts for use in assembly is also an example of excess inventory.

To reduce inventory, you can implement single-piece production, pull systems that call for the number of parts needed as they're needed, or kanban systems that signal when inventory needs to be replenished.

Overprocessing

Overprocessing occurs when unnecessary processes are performed on a component or product. Examples are adding an extra layer of varnish when one is sufficient and using two sheets of paper to wrap a completed product when one would do. You eliminate overprocessing by removing the unnecessary processing steps.

At an auto parts manufacturer, the team reviews its notes and the current-state value stream map, searching for areas of waste. Areas of waste it identifies include excess inventory, overproduction in the first process, and waiting in the second, third, and final processes.

So the team's analysis reveals several opportunities for improvement. The same type of analysis can be applied in service industries. Here examples of excess inventory are multiple copies of the same document, too many goods on a retail store shelf, or unnecessarily large stores of ingredients at a restaurant.

Examples of overprocessing are wrapping food or other retail products more than once, adding unnecessary features to a web site or software application, and any other task or feature that a customer doesn't want. Excess motion, as in the manufacturing industry, involves the unnecessary movement of employees. So in the service industry it could involve employees having to walk to another room to gather information.

Question

Suppose you're streamlining the sorting and delivery of food donations for a charity organization. You have created a current-state value stream map. Which are examples of actions you should perform next?

Options:

1. Note that tags are laboriously written up, which is a sign of overprocessing, and that this is because unnecessary information is currently required on the tags

2. Look for examples of overproduction and excess inventory – for example, foodstuffs are sorted quickly but then build up as inventory for the inspecting and tagging process

3. Review motion studies to determine if operators are walking or moving unnecessarily and find out why – for example, the sorting tables are positioned far from the tables where foodstuffs are inspected and tagged 4. Design a conveyor belt for moving sorted foodstuffs to speed up the tagging process

5. Ensure that each operator has a similar amount of work to do, to prevent bottlenecks in the process

Answer:

Option 1: This option is correct. Your first task is to identify waste and its causes. Here you notice an example of overprocessing and its possible cause.

Option 2: This is a correct option. You need to start by identifying waste – including overproduction and excess inventory – and determining its root causes, such as an unbalanced process flow.

Option 3: This option is correct. Your first task is to identify waste and its sources. In this example, you notice motion waste caused by poor layout of a work area.

Option 4: This option is incorrect. At this stage, it's too early to develop solutions to potential problems or inefficiencies. Instead you need to focus on identifying waste and its root causes.

Option 5: This is an incorrect option. Your first task is to identify waste and its causes. Line balancing is a strategy you could use later on, to address specific inefficiencies in the process.

IDENTIFYING PROCESS BLOCKS

Identifying process blocks

The second step in creating a future-state value stream map is to identify process blocks, which are processes or process steps for which cycle time exceeds takt time. Cycle time is the time it takes to complete a task, excluding any waiting or queuing time. Takt time is the time in which a task must be completed for production to continue at a rate that matches customer demand, given the work time that's available.

To calculate takt time, you divide the net operating time per period by customer requirements per period. To note bottlenecks per shift, you determine the number of working hours per shift, minus the time taken for breaks and meetings. This is the net operating time.

At the auto parts manufacturer, the team determines takt time as approximately 12 minutes. To do this, it divides the available time per shift – which is 7 hours, or 420 minutes – by the number of products the customer demands per shift, which is 35. A bottleneck is identified in the painting process because it has a cycle time of 14 minutes, which is over the calculated takt time of 12 minutes.

To identify process blocks, it's useful to create a bar chart of the time it takes to complete each process and to assess these times against takt time. If takt time is 15 minutes, the first and last processes in the example chart are bottlenecks because their cycle times exceed takt time.

Question

Suppose workers need to produce six products per one-hour shift to meet customer demand. Which process or processes in the bar chart represent bottlenecks?

The bar chart shows four processes. Process 1 has a cycle time of 10 minutes, Process 2 has a cycle time of 15 minutes, Process 3 has a cycle time of 12 minutes, and Process 4 has a cycle time of 9 minutes.

Options:

1. Process 2
2. Process 3
3. Process 1
4. Process 4

Answer:

Option 1: This option is correct. Process 2 has a cycle time of 15 minutes. Takt time, which you calculate in this example as 60 minutes divided by 6 units, is only 10 minutes. Processes that take longer than takt time represent bottlenecks.

Option 2: This option is correct. Takt time is work time divided by customer demand – in this example, it is 60 divided by 6, which equals 10 minutes. Process 3 has a cycle time that's over takt time by two minutes, so it represents a bottleneck.

Option 3: This option is incorrect. The cycle time for this process is exactly at takt time, which you calculate as 60 minutes divided by customer demand of 6 – or 10 minutes.

Option 4: This is an incorrect option. The cycle time for this process is one minute below takt time, so the process is likely to overproduce. Takt time is 60 minutes divided by customer demand of 6, or 10 minutes.

BALANCING PRODUCTION FLOW

Balancing production flow

Once you've identified process blocks, you can address these in one of two ways. For highly regulated and repeatable processes, you should implement line balancing. For less stable or regulated processes, you should implement a pull system, in which components are produced only as they're needed by the next process down the line.

The goal of line balancing is to ensure that work is shared evenly among all operators, with cycle times matching takt time. Line balancing involves noting the most frequent cycle times for each task within a process and creating an operator cycle time chart. Then you redistribute work and, if necessary, operators so that all tasks take about the same time to complete and can be done to takt time.

1. Note cycle times

A team identifies the most frequent times it takes operators to complete their tasks from the baseline data it gathers when creating a current-state map. For example, an operator responsible for applying a base coat of paint to a vehicle bumper typically takes 12 minutes to do this and the operator responsible for applying a top coat of paint takes 14 minutes on average. The team records these times as the relevant cycle times.

2. Create operator cycle time chart

After recording the cycle times, the team creates a cycle time chart. The vertical axis shows the number of minutes taken for each task recorded on the cycle time worksheet. The horizontal axis displays each operator. This chart should show the current state with the most frequent cycle times. You can also add a line depicting the takt time across the operator cycle time columns. A bar chart shows that applying a base coat of paint has a cycle time of 12 minutes and applying a top coat has a cycle time of 14 minutes. A line representing takt time is at 10 minutes.

3. Redistribute work

The aim of redistributing work is to ensure it's evenly distributed among operators, such that they can work to takt time. For example, this may mean re-assigning part of an operator's task to another operator, as well as changing the number of operators for a process.

The redistribution shown in the chart has the first and second operators working to takt time with the second operator helping apply base coats. Also, an additional operator has been brought in to take on extra work applying a top coat of paint. This operator is working to less than takt time and so may be assigned up to 4 minutes of additional work for a process further along the value stream.

A chart shows that the operator who applies a base coat of paint works for ten minutes, a second operator spends two minutes applying a base coat and 8 minutes applying a top coat of paint, and a third operator spends 6 minutes applying a top coat.

To reduce bottlenecks, you may need to bring in additional operators, or alter equipment or processes. In the auto parts example, an additional operator could remove the bottleneck. This method can also be used in the service industry for repeatable tasks such as data capture or system maintenance.

With predictable and repeatable processes, you can also remove bottlenecks by redesigning processes into one-piece flows. This involves merging two or more processes so that one seamless process results in a finished component or product. To do this, manufacturing areas are generally set up in U-shape designs with each task flowing to the next, without interruptions or work in process inventory. In the auto parts example, the fabrication, molding, and machining processes are combined into a single one-piece flow.

This dramatically reduces excess inventory, as well as required transport and waiting. One-piece flow design can also be useful in service environments. For example, in the food donation value stream map, the sort and tag process and the inspect process are separate. To improve flow, the sort and tag process can be combined with the inspect process. This will reduce the need for extra operators. It will also reduce waste in the form of waiting, transport, and motion.

Question

You're balancing the line for a press and assembly process at a manufacturing plant. Sequence the steps for doing this in the correct order.

Options:

A. Note that the press operator typically takes 80 seconds to add a new component and switch on the press

B. Create a bar chart showing cycle times for each operator

C. Add the inspection task to the press operator's workload so that she and the assembler have similar workloads

Answer:

Note that the press operator typically takes 80 seconds to add a new component and switch on the press is ranked the first step. Noting the most frequent times taken to complete tasks is the first step in line balancing.

Create a bar chart showing cycle times for each operator is ranked the second step. Using the most frequent times gathered in the first step, you create a bar chart showing the most frequent cycle times for each operator.

Add the inspection task to the press operator's workload so that she and the assembler have similar workloads is ranked the third step. To balance the line, you assess the chart made in the second step and redistribute work so that each operator has a similar workload and can work to takt time.

CREATING A PULL SYSTEM

Creating a pull system
When processes change often or aren't repeatable, it's best to implement a pull production system to balance the production line. Push systems move materials and information forward once a process is complete, irrespective of whether there's enough capacity to continue processing them at the next stage or there is a requirement of materials. In pull systems, the opposite applies – materials and information move only when they're needed by a process further down the line.

In a push system, if a client orders a batch of automobile bumpers, the order is sent to the first process in the production line – and the product is then pushed through each subsequent process. In a pull system, the customer's order is sent directly to the inspection process and the finished products are pulled from the inventory. The inspection process then pulls orders from the painting process.

To create pull systems, you typically use either post kanbans or signal kanbans. A kanban is a trigger that signals when inventory must be replenished. Kanbans can be used internally or to signal external suppliers.

Post kanban

Post kanbans typically involve using a two-card ordering system. One card is used when withdrawing inventory and another is used for ordering new stock. In value stream maps, a post kanban is typically depicted as an icon resembling a glass.

Signal kanban

Signal kanbans are visual signals that trigger replenishment. For example, two small bins of components may be kept. When one of the bins empties, it signals that the operator should refill it. Alternatively, sensors and lights can indicate when a particular inventory level is reached, signaling the need for more components from an earlier process.

In the auto part manufacturing example, the team creating a future-state value stream map plans the use of a post kanban to alert painters when they should fetch more vehicle bumpers from operators for the fabrication process. The team also plans to use signal kanbans, to signal staff whenever the inventory levels for the inspection and fabrication processes drop below a minimum threshold. The rectangles labeled "P" show that these are production kanbans, which signal the number of components to be produced by an upstream process.

Kaizen stars indicate the details of how the kanbans will work as part of a kaizen improvement initiative. The pull arrows in the future-state map indicate that the flow of products between suppliers, the manufacturing process, and customers will be based on the pull of customer demand.

Several other future-state icons are often used in value stream maps:
- supermarkets – a limited inventory controlled by kanbans. A supermarket is represented by an image of shelves that looks like a back-to-front capital letter "E."
- FIFO lanes – a predetermined limit for inventory between processes that follows the first-in-first-out rule. A FIFO lane is represented by a small square, circle, and triangle within two parallel lines. Above the top parallel line is the notation "Max = xx."
- U-shaped cells – the physical arrangement of the work area to accommodate one-piece flows. The U-shaped cell is represented as a square arch.

Remember the charity organization that donated food to local food banks. The future-state map for the targeted process has merged the sort and inspect and tag processes, with a FIFO lane between the supplier and the new, merged process. An inventory supermarket is set up between the sort, tag, and inspect process and the shipping and staging process. This should reduce the total inventory and limit overproduction.

Question

Suppose you're streamlining IV pump access and maintenance at a major hospital. You have created a current-state value stream map and now want to begin the process of creating a future-state map.

Which are examples of tasks you should perform?

Options:

1. Review why nurses have to walk long distances to retrieve IV pumps from storage

2. Calculate where cleaning, delivery, and setup processes for the IV pumps exceed takt time

3. Set up a kanban process to ensure cleaning and maintenance tasks are triggered when needed and

that IV bags are replaced before they empty, and show a post kanban icon on the map

4. Train nurses in new processes and ensure that pumps are stored next to each hospital bed

5. Time IV pump cleaning and maintenance tasks to gather baseline data

Answer:

Option 1: This option is correct. Analyzing the causes of existing waste, such as motion waste due to nurses walking long distances, is the first step in creating a future-state value stream map.

Option 2: This is a correct option. Once you've identified root causes of waste, you note where process bottlenecks are occurring by checking cycle times against takt time. Processes where cycle time is greater than takt time represent bottlenecks.

Option 3: This option is correct. Once you've identified waste and process bottlenecks, you balance the production line or implement a pull production system. In this example, kanbans are used to pull production.

Option 4: This option is incorrect. A future-state map identifies the future state you want to achieve, but not specific methods for achieving this state – like training personnel.

Option 5: This is an incorrect option. Gathering baseline data is a step you perform to create a current-state – rather than a future-state – map.

CHAPTER VI - APPLYING LEAN IN SERVICE AND MANUFACTURING ORGANIZATIONS

CHAPTER VI - Applying Lean in Service and Manufacturing Organizations
   SECTION 1 - Creating Lean Culture
   SECTION 2 - Cultural Change through Kaizen
   SECTION 3 - Implementing Kaizen in the Organization

SECTION 1 - CREATING LEAN CULTURE

SECTION 1 - Creating Lean Culture

For an organization to succeed in becoming Lean, it must adopt a Lean culture. This process is a lengthy one that requires good communication and top management support. Benefits of a Lean culture include lower employee turnover, greater adaptability and efficiency through rapid continuous improvements, more innovative solutions, and greater profitability.

An organization with a Lean culture has specific characteristics in terms of leadership, organizational structure, information management, employee-management relationships, and engineering.

BENEFITS OF LEAN CULTURE

Benefits of Lean culture

People often think of Lean as simply a group of tools you can use to maximize value and minimize waste. But a Lean organization also adopts a specific set of ideas about the workplace and its processes. And it performs ongoing assessments of how to minimize the use of production resources. An organization can minimize resource use by redesigning processes to eliminate waste. Some examples of waste include overprocessing, delays, downtime, defects, and excess inventory.

For the greatest benefits, though, this can't be a one-off effort. To become truly Lean, an organization has to internalize the Lean values and incorporate Lean methodologies in its standard practices. Therefore, it has to adopt a Lean culture. But what exactly makes up an organization's culture? For a start, its shared goals and values – as set out in the mission and value statements of the organization.

Culture is also revealed through behaviors – or what people typically do – as well as through norms, or generally accepted rules of behavior. These aren't written down, but people "understand" them – things like how to dress or what it's appropriate to say, or whether it's acceptable to interrupt superiors. An organization's underlying assumptions also contribute to its culture. These are the unconscious beliefs about the organization and those that work there. Examples of assumptions are that you have to win at all costs, or that employees need to help each other to solve daily problems.

Question

Think about your own organization. Do you have a clear idea of what your company's culture is?

Options:

1. Yes
2. A vague idea
3. No

Answer:

Option 1: You say you have a clear understanding of your company's culture. Your organization must communicate its shared goals and values well. A good understanding of an organization's mission and vision helps to clarify this aspect of organizational culture. Close attention to coworkers' behaviors, as well as their assumptions, can reveal more about the culture of an organization.

Option 2: You say you have a vague understanding of your company's culture. A good understanding of an organization's mission and vision helps to clarify its shared goals and values. Close attention to coworkers' behaviors and assumptions can reveal deeper aspects of the culture.

Option 3: You say you don't have a clear understanding of your company's culture. A good understanding of your organization's mission and vision will help you clarify its shared goals and values. If you pay close attention to your coworkers' behaviors and assumptions, they'll reveal deeper aspects of your company's culture.

Your company's culture plays an important role in its success. An example can illustrate this point. A group of friends in their twenties start a dot-com company. They aim to create a fun and laid-back culture, with an emphasis on perks and a creative work atmosphere.

The company's initial success is staggering, but eventually operational and staffing costs spiral out of control and the company goes under. In this case, the founders didn't have the managerial maturity or business acumen to create a sustainable business with a healthy, productive culture.

So a company's culture has a profound impact on the company's success and its sustainability. Given that changing company culture can be difficult, why make the shift to Lean? Adopting a Lean culture can have several benefits. It can result in lower employee turnover, motivated employees who generate rapid continuous improvements, and more innovative and team-directed solutions. Overall, it can mean greater profitability for an organization.

Lower employee turnover

In a Lean culture, employees have a greater sense of ownership of their work, as well as greater accountability. Teamwork and the generation of ideas for improvements are encouraged. Mistakes are typically seen as opportunities for learning and improvement, and the environment is supportive. In combination, these elements improve employee morale and so decrease employee turnover. This encourages a positive environment that helps everyone keep focused on meeting goals successfully.

Rapid continuous improvement

Lean companies actively encourage employees to identify problems and create solutions, which results in a greater number of improvement actions and greater adaptability. Everyone learns to accomplish more, without having to work harder. Strong internal teams and good communication strategies help sustain improvements and foster the culture of continuous improvement. Interactions are more supportive, improving the working environment.

Additionally, employees are rewarded for finding fault with current processes and generating solutions, rather than accepting that "this is just how things are done." Employees become the owners of their work.

Innovative and team-directed solutions

In a Lean culture, employees' suggestions for change are valued at all levels of the organization. This increases the number and diversity of employees working toward solutions. More innovative solutions are developed and employees have more say in how they perform their work. Leaders ask employees for solutions and teams direct their own solutions for their own problems.

Greater profitability

Reductions in employee turnover, high levels of employee motivation, and continuously improving processes and practices all have a positive effect on an organization's profitability. With frequent and innovative solutions, an organization uses fewer resources to provide the products or services its customers want. This is a win-

win situation for the organization, its employees, and its customers.

Question

What are the benefits of being able to create a Lean culture?

Options:

1. You will create a more positive work environment
2. Your working conditions and practices are continually improved and you work in supportive teams with good communication
3. You can be more innovative and have more ownership of your work
4. You help to create better results for your company
5. You are better able to understand hierarchical channels of communication because clearly defined roles exist at each level of the organizational hierarchy
6. You have a more relaxed and less disciplined workforce

Answer:

Option 1: This option is correct. In a Lean culture, all employees take ownership of their work and participate in generating ideas for improvements. This tends to result in happier, more motivated employees, and therefore in lower employee turnover.

Option 2: This is a correct option. Because everyone is involved in identifying problems and finding solutions, frequent and rapid improvement actions occur. Strong internal teams and effective communication sustain improvements, as well as fostering the culture of continuous improvement.

Option 3: This option is correct. Because of the greater number of problem-solvers involved, the improved communication, and the supportive team environment, solutions in a Lean organization tend to be more innovative and change is more sustainable. You have a direct say in what you do and in improving your working conditions.

Option 4: This is a correct option. In a Lean culture, motivated employees, continuous improvements, and team-led innovation all lead to greater profitability for an organization. This in turn leads to greater job security and pride in your company.

Option 5: This is an incorrect option. An organization's hierarchy typically becomes flatter with the adoption of a Lean culture, which emphasizes the accountability of all employees for their work.

Option 6: This option is incorrect. A Lean culture is supportive but highly disciplined, with an emphasis on efficiency and the ongoing assessment of processes.

CHARACTERISTICS OF LEAN CULTURE

Characteristics of Lean culture

Changing over to a Lean way of thinking can be difficult. Estimates state that a majority of companies fail to implement Lean successfully. Similarly, it's estimated that between 10 and 20% of leaders are unable or unwilling to make the change to Lean. So why is this the case? Often, it's because organizations adopt Lean tools and practices, but fail to adopt a Lean organizational culture. If Lean principles aren't assimilated at every level of the organization, your chances for a successful Lean enterprise are slim.

The concept of switching to a Lean culture can be intimidating for organizations because it requires a fairly radical change in metrics and behaviors. Additionally, because the culture is one of continuous improvement, it's something that can't be achieved through a one-off drive. It requires daily practice and long-term commitment.

When attempting to adopt a Lean culture, it's important to remember that your organization's current culture probably developed over many years. Lean culture will require employees, who are settled in their ways of thinking and doing things, to change. It can sometimes take near disaster to get them to consider something new.

Additionally, once people are willing to embrace change, you need patience. A Lean culture, like any other, takes years to develop. The change requires the support of top management and should have a concerted and consistent communication strategy. All of a company's work processes and communications will affect its success.

Key areas of difference between Lean and traditional "non-Lean" organizational cultures can be found in the categories of leadership, organizational structure, information management, employee-management relations, and engineering.

Leadership

Non-Lean leadership relies heavily on executive commands being followed to the letter by employees lower down the hierarchy. In a Lean culture, leaders provide vision and encourage participation at all levels. Tactical decisions are delegated to workers, while leaders guide strategy. Leaders in a Lean culture stretch employees to encourage development and try to distribute work fairly and evenly so that employees aren't overloaded.

Organizational structure

Typical non-Lean organizations have hierarchical structures with top-down communication. Employees are expected to do what they're told and may be penalized for mistakes. Lean organizational structures are more flat and include cross-functional teams. This encourages initiative at all levels and promotes bi-directional information flow.

Information management

In non-Lean environments, information management relies strongly on abstract reports. For instance, reports are textual and often rely on estimates and forecasts. With Lean, teams maintain visual control systems which provide rich information sources. For example, a board containing cards may show exactly where all items are in a production system, at any point. Communication is expected to be timely and thorough, providing tactical details of what actions are required and when they should be completed.

Employee-management relations

Non-Lean culture values loyalty and obedience in employee-management relations. Relations may be strained as a result of alienation or labor disputes. When errors occur, blame is typically assigned to a "fall person." Lean culture values close involvement and sharing of ideas between employees and management. Employees are encouraged to challenge practices and communication processes to bolster innovation. Error reporting is valued as an opportunity for all to learn.

Engineering

In non-Lean culture, engineering is typically isolated from the customer and the production floor. With Lean culture, a cross-functional team-based model is used. Input from the customer is encouraged at all stages. Product and production design occur concurrently in collaboration with key stakeholders.

Suppose an employee is working on a production floor, sanding wood for kitchen unit installations. The employee has been told to stop work and call a supervisor if he notices a defect or if he makes a mistake. As the person sands, his hand slips and he creates a deep scratch in the wood.

In a non-Lean culture, the supervisor reprimands the employee and reminds him that the wood is expensive. This is an unpleasant experience and one that's likely to encourage the employee to hide mistakes in future. In a Lean culture, the supervisor shows the employee a better way to hold the sander to avoid slips in future.

The mistake is discussed in a briefing meeting at the end of the shift. Other workers and the supervisor applaud the worker for stopping work, admitting the mistake, and providing an opportunity to improve standard training in sander use. By reworking your organization's approach to leadership, organizational structure, information management, employee-management relationships, and engineering, you can begin to instill a new Lean culture. But remember that this process takes time and should be integrated slowly.

Question

Match each characteristic to the corresponding type of organizational culture. More than one characteristic may match to a type.

Options:

A. Leaders ask employees to find a way to implement a strategy

B. Cross-functional teams collaborate for product types

C. An executive directive about quality processes is executed

D. Designers work in their offices and put designs through to the production floor

E. Employees say a brief meeting at the end of the shift would work better than a weekly one

F. Managers feed process changes to employees
Targets:
1. Lean
2. Non-Lean
Answer:
In Lean culture, leaders provide strategy and direction, but cross-functional teams of employees make tactical decisions and collaborate with one another. Organizational structure is relatively flat, and all employees are encouraged to question and improve existing processes.

In traditional, non-Lean cultures, employees are expected to follow executive directives without question. Communication is largely unidirectional and occurs from the top down. Engineering – or design – is separated from both the customers and production workers.

SECTION 2 - CULTURAL CHANGE THROUGH KAIZEN

SECTION 1 - Cultural Change through Kaizen

Kaizen culture incorporates the ideal of continuous improvement, embracing change that adds value for the customer. To encourage and sustain this culture, you need to ensure all employees understand the change processes, provide leadership commitment, and develop an infrastructure that supports continuous improvement.

A useful method for integrating kaizen culture in the workforce is to use kaizen events to identify waste and implement improvements to the value stream. Key characteristics of kaizen events are that they're value-stream driven, have stretch objectives for eliminating waste, require cross-functional teams and employee involvement, and are short in duration.

WHY A KAIZEN CULTURE?

Why a kaizen culture?

Kaizen is a continuous improvement practice and philosophy. In Japanese, "kai" translates as "change" and "zen" translates as "good." This entails taking something apart and putting it back together in a better way. So the kaizen principle involves changing current practices to make them better. This principle requires everyone to assess and solve problems, enabling them to meet customer demand with less effort and fewer resources.

Practicing kaizen encourages Lean thinking and culture. It involves all employees taking ownership of their work and finding ways to make it more efficient and effective. The more employees practice kaizen, the more familiar Lean thinking becomes. So how do manufacturing and service industries apply kaizen?

Service

An insurance company discovers that explaining a product to a client and signing the relevant papers for a sale takes nearly an hour. A team of sales people, lawyers, and finance employees review the documentation and the key aspects of the company's biggest-selling insurance product. In a week, they're able to reduce the pitch and signing time to five minutes – freeing up their and their customers' time.

Manufacturing

A manufacturing company finds that changing a metal die press to a new size takes almost three hours. The long changeover time creates bottlenecks in production. It becomes more economical to produce large batch sizes – despite an increase in storage and transportation requirements. Engineers and factory workers get together to determine how to reduce the changeover time. Together they develop a new system that reduces it to only 20 minutes.

These examples highlight some of the reasons why organizations should use kaizen. It produces fast results, and can lead to improved productivity and lower costs. In addition, an indirect benefit of this approach is higher employee morale.

Fast results

Using kaizen, your organization can make multiple, small improvements to address a range of relatively minor problems. Kaizen-based modifications that are timely and cost-effective provide visible benefits at all levels of the organization. In turn, this helps build support for the change to Lean at all levels.

Improved productivity

Because kaizen focuses on eliminating waste, processes begin to have faster turnaround times, quality improves, and productivity increases. This means that customers receive better quality products without delays. In turn, satisfied customers support your organization's products and its reputation improves. So successful kaizen initiatives lead to greater customer loyalty and increased market share.

Lower costs

In manufacturing industries, reducing waste through kaizen often leads to less inventory and more streamlined production with fewer errors. So companies spend less on resources to achieve similar or better production figures. In the service industry, flexibility in dealing with changing customer demands is vital. So getting things right the first time is a key goal. Kaizen focuses on this, helping to reduce extra work caused by initial failures to meet customer demands or expectations.

Higher employee morale

When employees take ownership of their work and when work stress is relieved through improved work practices, employees' morale improves. Kaizen also helps to encourage interdepartmental communication and builds employees' expertise beyond their specific tasks. This helps employees to make better and more informed decisions and to solve problems more effectively. Finally, as employee morale improves, the reputation of the organization as an employer of choice grows and it begins to attract further talent.

Kaizen means employees can practice identifying waste and using Lean tools to eliminate it. As employees learn experientially and produce tangible results, they become more confident in their abilities and authority to make Lean improvements. This process takes time. There's no magic way to create an instant cultural shift – but the more you do something, the more familiar you become with Lean, until eventually it's routine.

Question

How ready do you think your organization is to adopt a kaizen culture?

Options:

1. Completely ready
2. Moderately ready
3. Not ready

Answer:

Option 1: You say your organization is completely ready to adopt a kaizen culture. Although confidence is great, the process is complex and takes time. Keep things moving slowly and surely, and use the information in the next section to help guide your organization's transition to a kaizen culture.

Option 2: You say your organization is moderately ready to adopt a kaizen culture. The process is complex and slow, so making small steps is the way forward. Use the information in the next section to help guide your organization toward a kaizen culture.

Option 3: You say your organization is not ready to adopt a kaizen culture. Consider the strategies outlined in the next section. You may be able to apply them in your organization to begin the shift toward a kaizen culture.

STRATEGIES FOR CULTURE CHANGE

Strategies for culture change

As most people learn, creating effective change is difficult. It may start off well, but its often difficult to maintain. For example, people often begin a new diet or exercise program with enthusiasm, or at least determination. But over time they run out of steam, ultimately going back to their old routines.

But that doesn't mean change can't succeed. Perhaps from your own experience of successful change, you can isolate the factors that kept you going and helped you to accept and embrace something new. Experts have developed three key strategies to ensure kaizen becomes a permanent part of an organization's culture. These strategies are to explain the change process, provide leadership commitment, and develop an infrastructure that supports continuous improvement.

By clearly explaining the change process, you help ensure employees understand and embrace the need for change. To do this effectively, you need to use motivation techniques, as well as provide guidance and the necessary skills to implement the required changes.

Motivation

External motivations such as pay increases tend to have a short-term effect in providing incentives for change. Typically, intrinsic motivations have a longer and more sustainable impact in driving change. So providing intrinsic motivations, such as a sense of inclusion and control, is key to sustaining changes in behavior.

With kaizen, cross-functional teams address this need for inclusion. Giving employees authority to improve their work environment provides them with a sense of control. However, asking employees for improvement ideas and then not trying them out will undermine this.

Guidance

Leaders need to make it clear why the change is necessary and to set measurable objectives so that progress can be measured. To provide guidance, leaders should create a clearly defined action plan, which clarifies expectations, time frames, and accountability.

Without clear action plans, employees become confused and frustrated when facing change. You lower the intrinsic stress of change when you guide others so they know what to do and when to do it in a new situation.

Skills

Facilitators teach Lean tools and concepts, monitor improvement initiatives, and provide feedback to all involved. Additionally, because learning by doing – also known as experiential learning – is encouraged, retention of newly learned skills is high. Without practice, kaizen thinking isn't likely to become integrated into an organization's culture.

The cliche "actions speak louder than words" holds true for leaders who hope to inspire commitment to a Lean culture. Leaders need to be involved and be seen implementing the changes themselves. This helps employees understand that this change is meant to last and they need to embrace it.

Leaders should be actively engaged in planning, and attend briefings and team presentations. By being there and actively working with teams, leaders inspire employees to embrace the change. Leaders need to adjust to rapid decision making, giving frontline workers the authority to make tactical changes. If leaders don't allow this, they undermine kaizen culture and employees aren't given the opportunity to take ownership of their work.

Leaders need to understand that not every experiment will work and that they need to carefully monitor each attempted improvement. To develop an infrastructure that supports continuous improvement, organizations must provide sufficient personnel and oversight of improvement initiatives.

Personnel

It's recommended that organizations have one full-time Lean employee for every 100 workers. This employee is responsible for coordinating and providing strategic direction for improvement actions. The employee should also work with top management to remove any blocks to integrating kaizen culture. Typically, organizations can support four structured and intensive improvement initiatives per 100 employees per year.

Oversight

Leaders should assess which improvements to prioritize, facilitate improvement initiatives – such as value stream mapping - and monitor processes to ensure sustainability. They should also provide ongoing Lean training to employees at all levels.

To succeed at integrating kaizen thinking in your organization, you need to have all three strategies in place and they must all be working well.

Question

Which actions and strategies should you use to build a kaizen culture?

Options:

1. Explain the change process
2. Provide leadership commitment
3. Develop an infrastructure that supports continuous improvement
4. Set up penalties for non-compliance
5. Initiate a series of executive-defined actions for employees to practice

Answer:

Option 1: This is a correct option. By understanding the components that make up a successful change process – motivation, guidance, and skills – you're better able to sustain and integrate the change to a kaizen culture.

Option 2: This option is correct. To encourage the adoption of a kaizen culture, leaders need to demonstrate their commitment and support employee-initiated tactical decision making.

Option 3: This is a correct option. Ensuring that dedicated personnel administer improvement initiatives provides an infrastructure that supports continuous improvement. This helps to sustain commitment.

Option 4: This option is incorrect. A punitive environment is less effective than a supportive one.

Change is often difficult for people, and they need support and guidance.

Option 5: This is an incorrect option. To encourage a kaizen culture, executives should provide overall strategy, but employees should be encouraged to make tactical decisions regarding their work.

CHARACTERISTICS OF KAIZEN EVENTS

Characteristics of kaizen events

A kaizen event is an improvement initiative in which employees from various departments come together to analyze a problem. Employees work in cross-functional teams to identify waste, propose solutions, and implement changes. The aim is to shift organizational culture while enhancing specific processes.

These examples of kaizen events may be directed at improving a specific process or reducing a specific type of waste:
- finding ways to smooth out workflow using line balancing in a production plant,
- applying 5S in an office workspace, removing clutter and rearranging equipment to eliminate wasted motion, and
- changing to electronic databases in an office or to a visual kanban information stream in a factory to improve information flow.

Kaizen events share certain characteristics. They are value-stream driven, have stretch objectives for eliminating waste, require cross-functional teams and employee involvement, and are short in duration.

Question

Which two characteristics do you think are connected to the characteristic of kaizen events being value-stream driven?

Options:

1. Kaizen events involve using cross-functional teams
2. Kaizen focuses on waste elimination
3. Kaizen teams focus on improvement
4. Kaizen events are strategic rather than tactical

Answer:

Option 1: This is a correct option. Because people from different areas of the value stream share ideas and information, the team has a broader perspective of the value stream.

Option 2: This option is correct. Value is defined as what a customer is willing to pay for, so by eliminating waste, you focus on value-add activities within the value stream.

Option 3: This option is incorrect. Improvement efforts are generally well-intentioned but often fall short because the entire value stream isn't considered or understood. Wanting to improve processes is not enough.

Option 4: This is an incorrect option. Kaizen events are tactical methods for implementing strategy.

Lean and kaizen identify value from the customer's perspective. This challenges kaizen teams to make improvements that have a direct impact on the customer's experience. To help ensure the full value stream is analyzed, kaizen events are typically linked to future-state value stream maps.

A second characteristic of kaizen events is their stretch objectives. Each event's objectives should be based on ideal performance measures rather than on historical performance. These objectives should be measurable and should "stretch" everyone so that they perform at their best.

Typically the aim is to remove waste rather than to improve value-add activities. This should provide clear direction for the outcomes of a kaizen event. The waste areas targeted should be ones that will provide the greatest impact or the most immediate results. This is because achieving rapid positive results encourages further kaizen events and embeds kaizen culture more fully into the workforce.

A cross-functional team in a kaizen event may comprise upstream and downstream frontline workers, subject matter experts, Lean facilitators, and even external suppliers and customers. The benefits of using such a diverse team include reducing interpersonal tensions, improving the value stream, and increasing the knowledge base.

Reducing interpersonal tensions

Bringing together people from different departments promotes a better understanding of different stakeholders' needs. Also, solving problems as members of a team builds personal bonds, reducing interdepartmental and interpersonal tensions.

Improving the value stream

By working together on a defined issue, team members gain a fuller understanding of the target process and what its real needs are. This helps to ensure that improvements impact the entire value stream.

Increasing the knowledge base

During the kaizen event, team members learn about the steps that make up the entire process and about how customer value affects process design. The team practices analyzing a process, and planning and implementing an improvement. This provides the group with new or additional skills. Also, through this experiential form of learning, team members gain confidence in their authority and capabilities in terms of tactical decision making. Finally, kaizen events give managers practice in letting go of tactical decision making and trusting frontline workers with these decisions.

The key members on a kaizen team are the frontline employees who work on the targeted process daily. In traditional environments, these workers don't receive the opportunity to explore their ideas for what could improve their work.

Kaizen ensures that changes aren't made by a single expert, but by team members. This increases the number of minds and perspectives brought to bear on a problem. As a result, there's greater innovation. And because the process is more inclusive, the solutions developed are more sustainable.

The final characteristic of a kaizen event is its short duration. This is accomplished by having a team working full-time on the issue so it can focus entirely on it. Kaizen events typically have a duration of only two to five days. In this short time, they may nevertheless provide substantial benefits for an organization.

Question

Match the characteristics of a kaizen event to their descriptions.

Options:

A. Value-stream driven
B. Stretch objectives
C. Employee involvement
D. Cross-functional teams
E. Short duration

Targets:

1. The focus is on removing waste from a process
2. Performance levels are set at what should be possible, rather than what has been possible in the past
3. Frontline workers generate improvement ideas and are closely involved in implementing these ideas
4. Teams comprise employees, experts, suppliers, and customers who focus on the entire value stream
5. Events typically last two to five days, where teams focus entirely on the event and don't carry out their usual duties

Answer:

Kaizen events are value-stream driven because they focus on removing waste – which is defined from the customer's perspective – from the entire value stream, often using a future-state value stream map to plan improvements

Stretch objectives are based on what performance levels should be rather than on what they have been. This encourages high performance.

In a kaizen event, employees get involved by using their knowledge to generate improvement ideas and put these ideas into practice.

Cross-functional teams use employees from upstream and downstream processes as well as experts, customers, and suppliers. This broadens the available knowledge base and ensures the event is value-stream driven.

Kaizen events are generally short in duration, lasting two to five days. During this time teams are sequestered so they can focus on the improvement activity and aren't expected to continue with their normal work duties.

SECTION 3 - IMPLEMENTING KAIZEN IN THE ORGANIZATION

SECTION 3 - Implementing Kaizen in the Organization

When planning a kaizen event, you need to choose a target process or area for improvement, assemble a cross-functional team, and draw up an event charter. The charter provides details of the event's scope, of the kaizen team, and of the event schedule.

To run a kaizen event once it has been planned, a team begins by gathering baseline data through observation of the target process or area. Using this data, it identifies waste in the target and finds its root causes.

The team then brainstorms improvement ideas, and prioritizes and tests these ideas. It then develops appropriate staff training, implements the agreed improvements, and monitors the results.

PLANNING A KAIZEN EVENT

Planning a kaizen event

Careful planning is essential for any kaizen event – without a good plan, you won't achieve results. When planning a kaizen event, you need to select a target for the event. This may be a specific process or site. Then you select event leaders who'll provide oversight for the core kaizen team. Finally, you draw up an event charter to provide details of the event's scope, objectives, logistics, and of who is accountable for different aspects of the event.

When choosing a target site or process, you need to consider the organization's strategic goals, what could eliminate the most waste or costs, and what benefits the event could have on the organization's profits.

For example, you may create a rating table to determine which of two processes to target at a large manufacturer. One is the die casting process and the other is the product assembly process for a specific product family. Follow along as the rating table is used to select the best of a set of potential targets for a kaizen event.

You add key business drivers that you want the kaizen event to address. You also add kaizen event drivers. Then you add a Totals and an Average row for later calculations.

Next you determine a rating scale for how the event is likely to impact the business driver or kaizen target. Typically, the scale should be kept as simple as possible.

You add ratings for each process. In this example, the die cast process scores high for most business drivers, but scores very low on the kaizen event drivers of fast results, risk, and cost.

You then calculate totals and averages for each process. In this case, the die cast process adds up to a total of 15, with an average of 2.5. The total of the assemble and pack process is 19; its average is 3.17.

Using the rating table, the manufacturer determines that it needs to target the assemble and pack process. This process has the potential to deliver more overall benefits to the organization after improvement and makes a good target for a kaizen event. Once you've selected a target process to improve, you need to appoint event leaders to champion the event. These should include a Lean facilitator, as well as an executive sponsor, a value stream champion, a team lead, and an event coordinator.

These leaders should meet regularly during the planning process to monitor progress and provide necessary resources. The facilitator will direct the selection of members for a cross-functional team.

THE EVENT CHARTER

The event charter

Once a cross-functional team is in place, the next step is to develop a kaizen event charter. This document is updated and goes through several reviews before the planning process completes and the event can begin. It outlines the scope of the event, the team's membership, and the schedule for the event.

In the event scope section, you identify the value stream that you're working on. For example, this might be "engineering change notice process," "recruitment," or, as in this scenario, "Series 7 Electronic." You also name the event, based on the process it's designed to improve.

Scope-narrowing information includes any factors used to narrow scope, such as location, customer, and product. In the manufacturing example, this is the product type – portable stereo. The trigger is the activity that signals work to begin. For example, this may be receipt of an order or the delivery of components.

Next you record the first step and the final step of the process that the kaizen event is targeting. Here this is "attach handle" and "pack." Then you document any limitations. For instance, the team isn't authorized to change the box size for packaging. To complete the scope section of the kaizen event charter, you record event drivers and current issues, objectives, deliverables, and obstacles.

Drivers and current issues

In the drivers and current issues section, you list up to five reasons why the kaizen event is needed. Examples could be increases in defects or customer complaints, late deliveries, market demands, and cost increases.

Objectives

The objectives section should set measurable objectives for the kaizen event. Examples might be to reduce production time from five to three days, reduce errors by 25%, or increase productivity by 20%.

Deliverables

If you know what the deliverables may be at this stage, record them. However, try to ensure this doesn't dictate how the team should make improvements. For example, if you specify the use of line balancing, the team may feel unable to consider other potential solutions.

Obstacles

Obstacles are any circumstances or events that could pull team members from their kaizen duties or prevent the event from being a success. Examples of potential obstacles are equipment failure and resistance to change.

When selecting the core team, you need six to eight members who currently perform the targeted process or are representatives from upstream or downstream areas of the value stream. In the manufacturing example, three assembly and packing employees, a components manufacturer representative, and a shipping representative are selected. The sixth member of the team is the facilitator.

The facilitator trains the other team members in Lean tools and concepts, and prepares them to gather data, identify waste, and implement solutions. The scheduling and logistics aspect of the kaizen events charter includes dates, start and end times, location, interim briefing dates, staff training, and the date and time of the team presentation.

Dates and start and end times

The work should be planned for consecutive days in shifts of eight or more hours, depending on the industry. In service environments, eight hours is recommended. In some manufacturing environments, longer shifts may be needed.

If the team will be mapping processes, allow a couple of days for mapping and around three days for improvement design. Time for training the workforce in the new process also needs to be factored in. In the manufacturing example, dates are given as August 2 to 6. The start time is given as 8:30 a.m. and the end time is given as 5:00 p.m.

Location

The team should be assigned an on-site room, large enough to accommodate the full team and with wall space for mapping and other visual tools. Typically, the larger the space, the better. In the manufacturing example, the event charter indicates that the team has been assigned conference room 3.

Interim briefings

Interim briefings should be planned for the final hour of the shift on every second day. The team may not need this number of meetings, but it's best to schedule time in case it does. The interim briefings for the manufacturing team are scheduled for August 2, 4, and 6.

Training

The staff training schedule is often left as tentative in the planning stages because the content of the training is unknown. The number of people to be trained may also be unknown. It should, however, be completed before the end of the event. The Staff training section in the kaizen charter has TBD entered into it.

Presentation

The team presentation is generally set for the final hour of the kaizen event. If physical improvements have occurred, it may be useful to include a walkthrough in which others can be shown the improvements. The Team presentation is scheduled for 4:00 p.m. on August 6.

Question

A call center wants to implement a kaizen event to improve its operations and promote a Lean culture.

Which activities should be performed while planning the kaizen event?

Options:

1. Rate the customer data entry and complaint-handling processes against a list of key business drivers

2. Approach the departmental head to be the executive sponsor for the kaizen event

3. Create a document detailing issues such as the objective to reduce customer waiting times by 25% and the event schedule

4. Video tape the current customer data entry process to gather baseline data

5. Discuss potential database improvements with the IT department

Answer:

Option 1: This option is correct. During planning, a target process must be selected for improvement. Using a rating system is an effective way of identifying the best target.

Option 2: This is a correct option. During planning, members of the kaizen team must be selected. This includes team leaders such as the executive sponsor, value-stream champion, facilitator, team lead, and event coordinator.

Option 3: This option is correct. Event leaders need to create a kaizen event charter during the planning phase. This document outlines the scope of the event, details of the team, and the schedule for the event.

Option 4: This option is incorrect. If baseline data doesn't already exist, the core team could carry out this activity as part of the event itself, rather than as a planning activity.

Option 5: This is an incorrect option. This discussion would be part of the event itself, and it's likely that a member of the IT department would be part of the core kaizen team.

IDENTIFYING CAUSES OF WASTE

Identifying causes of waste

Using the plan created in the kaizen event charter, you can begin to implement the kaizen event to improve a work process. The first two steps in this four-step process are to gather baseline data through observation and to identify waste and its root causes. The final two steps are to brainstorm ideas for improvement and to implement the improvements.

Using video taping or photographs, you observe and record the current process. Your aim is to gain a full understanding of the process and to gather data such as cycle time, defect rate, and number of operators so you can develop current maps of the process. The team may need a selection of tools for gathering data and using it to create visual maps.

Tools

Useful tools for creating baseline data include cycle time flow charts, operator cycle time charts, time observation sheets, Pareto charts, and analysis of variance tools. In the manufacturing example, the team uses time observation sheets and operator cycle time charts to gather baseline data.

Maps

Once the data is gathered, you can create current state value-stream maps, 5S maps, workflow analysis maps, and cycle time flow charts. Using the data gathered, the manufacturing kaizen team creates a current-state value stream map of the process. It also creates a 5S map of the assembly and packing area.

Once the baseline data has been gathered, team members identify waste in the process, along with its causes. To do this, they can categorize steps as value-adding or non-value adding, and check for issues such as waiting and unnecessary motion. You can use different tools to analyze the root causes of the waste you identify. These tools include the 5 Whys process, cause-and-effect diagrams, Pareto charts, and checksheets.

For example, the 5 Whys tool requires that you question why waste occurs and keep questioning until you find the root cause of the problem. The kaizen team at the electronics manufacturer notices that operators spend a lot of time waiting for components to arrive and that some then have to wait while the first operator completes a task. The team also notices that operators make unnecessary movements, bending and searching for tools and packing materials.

To analyze what is causing these wastes, the team questions why the operators need to wait and why they have to move around so much. It determines that the operators receive components on a push system, that the cycle times for their respective tasks are different – with the result that the line is unbalanced - and that the layout of their work area is inefficient.

Team members are a little anxious that if they conduct line balancing, some of the operators could lose their jobs. The facilitator reassures the team that if only two operators are needed, additional workers will be redeployed.

Question

A kaizen team for a financial auditing firm has completed the planning stage for a kaizen event. It has decided to target the company's acquisition audit process.

Which actions should the team take to start running the kaizen event?

Options:

1. The team works backward through the target process, recording actions and the time it takes to complete them

2. The team questions why the audit reports take so long to be approved

3. The team notices that the audit includes categories that aren't required by regulations

4. The team schedules interim briefing sessions for the last hour of every second day of the event

5. The team creates a future state value-stream map to include the improved process they've tested

Answer:

Option 1: This option is correct. Working through the process and recording times is part of the baseline data gathering process and is typically the first step in a kaizen event.

Option 2: This is a correct option. Analyzing the root causes of identified wastes – such as the long cycle time for the audit report approval process – is an aspect of the second step in running a kaizen event, which is identifying waste and its root causes.

Option 3: This option is correct. Identifying unnecessary audit categories is an example of identifying waste. This is an aspect of the second step in running a kaizen event, which is identifying waste and its root causes.

Option 4: This option is incorrect. The team should schedule interim briefing sessions for the final hour of every second day during the planning stage. It might not need to meet at each scheduled session, but it's good practice to have a meeting room set aside for these times.

Option 5: This option is incorrect. Planning and implementing solutions is the next step in the process. The first two steps involve gathering baseline data and identifying waste and its root causes. At this stage, the team would create a current state value-stream map to provide an overview of the current process.

BRAINSTORM AND IMPLEMENT IMPROVEMENTS

Brainstorm and implement improvements

Once waste and its root causes have been identified, the team needs to brainstorm ideas for improvement and then find a way to implement these improvements. During brainstorming, the team reviews the current state map and searches for ways to improve it. All ideas are welcomed during an initial non-judgmental process.

The kaizen team for the electronics manufacturer is targeting a specific electronic product and the final assembly process for that product. The team identified waiting, motion, and unbalanced lines as key wastes. It proposes a kanban system, 5S, line balancing, and the use of standardized work to improve the process.

Other ideas include using taller work tables to minimize bending and using inventory trolleys on wheels so that operators don't have to walk to the stores to gather materials as frequently. The team must then evaluate and prioritize the improvement ideas it has generated. It creates drafts, samples, maps, or prototypes of the planned improvements for testing. This process is similar in both service and manufacturing environments.

Service

In the service industry, testing may include a test-run for new client-entry processes or reviewing draft work checklists or other aids. In terms of changes to office layout, this may be done using software programs, drawings, or even cardboard models.

Manufacturing

In the manufacturing industry, testing may include reviewing specifications on new equipment, creating a prototype of a different component, or having an operator attempt a new standardized work process.

Once you've tested the proposed solutions and determined which you want to use, you move to the implementation step. You now need to consider staff training and develop a schedule for going live with the improvement.

Staff training

To develop appropriate staff training, the team needs to consider exactly what workers need to do and what they need to know if they are to implement the improvement correctly. Downstream or upstream operators may also need to be trained. So you need to clarify who should be trained, how long this training will take, and what it should cover.

Schedule

The schedule needs to be updated with the training schedule. This may mean shifting the date of the team presentation. It's best to schedule the new process to be implemented in the workplace at the start of a day or when workers begin their shift. It's best to schedule the new process to be implemented in the workplace at the start of a day or when workers begin their shift.

The kaizen team for the electronics manufacturer prioritized the use of 5S, line balancing, and kanban to improve the assemble and pack process. The team tests the potential layout for the area using sticky notes for each piece of furniture in the area. This is part of their 5S strategy.

The team uses an operator cycle chart to balance the line. It then tests the result using two operators. For the kanban solution, the team rigs flashing lights to component trolleys. On each trolley, the light can be switched on when the component stack reaches a painted line.

Testing the brainstormed solutions is key to assessing their value before the changes are rolled out. Once this is done, the implementation process can begin – starting with staff training. When assessing what to cover in staff training, the team realizes that operators need to know where everything is located after the 5S initiative. The operators must also know what they need to do in terms of assembly and packing tasks in the new balanced line.

Finally, the operators supplying components for this process need to know what to do when the kanban is triggered. Once everyone is prepared, the team rolls out the new process, at the planned start date of August 12. The team also needs to follow up the kaizen event. This includes regular monitoring of results and improvements, creating standards, and communicating results and process audits. This helps to solidify the new process and may highlight further improvement needs.

Question

A kaizen team at a call center plans to streamline a data-entry process. Sequence the examples of the team's activities during the kaizen event in order.

Options:

A. Go through recordings of new client conversations and time operators' entries into the customer database

B. Notice that the database is slow to load, that more information than is required is being entered, and that a high number of data errors are occurring

C. Consider using different database software, upgrading operators' computers, and editing the question script for the process

D. Train call center operators in the new process and implement the agreed improvements

Answer:

Go through recordings of new client conversations and time operators' entries into the customer database is ranked the first step. The first step is to gather baseline data by observing the process and timing each task in the process.

Notice that the database is slow to load, that more information than is required is being entered, and that a high number of data errors are occurring is ranked the second step. The second step involves identifying waste and its root causes. In this case, waiting, errors, and overprocessing are problems caused by slow database loading, the question list, and a lack of failsafes to prevent data errors.

Consider using different database software, upgrading operators' computers, and editing the question script for the process is ranked the third step. The third step is to brainstorm ideas, prioritize solutions, and test these solutions. In this case, the team considers equipment and software upgrades, as well as changes to the process itself, as potential solutions.

Train call center operators in the new process and implement the agreed improvements is ranked the fourth step. The fourth step is training staff and implementing the best solutions.

REFERENCES

References
1. **Lean For Dummies** - 2007, Natalie J. Sayer and Bruce Williams, John Wiley & Sons
2. **Lean Office Demystified: Using the Power of the Toyota Production System in Your Administrative Areas** - 2006, Don Tapping and Anne Dunn, MCS Media
3. **The New Lean Pocket Guide XL: Tools for the Elimination of Waste!** - 2005, Don Tapping, MCS Media
4. **Lean Maintenance** - 2008, Joel Levitt, Industrial Press
5. **Transactional Six Sigma and Lean Servicing: Leveraging Manufacturing Concepts to Achieve World-Class Service** - 2002, Betsi Harris Ehrlich, St. Lucie Press
6. **Creating Your Lean Future State: How to Move from Seeing to Doing** - 2006, Tom Luyster, Don Tapping, Productivity Press

7. **Lean Assembly: The Nuts and Bolts of Making Assembly Operations Flow** - 2002, Michel Baudin, Productivity Press
8. **Lean Manufacturing that Works: Powerful Tools for Dramatically Reducing Waste and Maximizing Profits** - 2005, Bill Carreira, AMACOM
9. **The Kaizen Event Planner: Achieving Rapid Improvement in Office, Service, and Technical Environments** - 2007, Karen Martin and Mike Osterling, Productivity Press
10. **Toyota Culture: The Heart and Soul of the Toyota Way** - 2008, Jeffrey K. Liker, Michael Hoseus, The Center for Quality People and Organizations, McGraw-Hill
11. **Lean Production Simplified: A Plain-Language Guide to the World's Most Powerful Production System, 2nd Edition** - 2007, Pascal Dennis, Productivity Press

GLOSSARY

Glossary
   A
   action plan - A scheduled plan describing specific goals and actions that will be taken to meet them.
   andon - An electronic signaling device that conveys information, such as impending danger or process status.
   B
   Black Belt - A professional trained in Six Sigma methodologies and principles who usually leads improvement projects.
   bottleneck - A situation in which products are processed too slowly at one stage in a production process so that they accumulate upstream, waiting to be processed.
   brainstorm - An interactive group process during which creative ideas are generated.
   C
   continuous improvement - The ongoing and incremental improvement of processes, products, or services.

cross-functional team - A team made up of employees who perform different functions and have different skills.

current state (value stream) map - A graphical and chronological representation of how processes, information, and resources flow in the value stream at the time of being mapped.

customer - A person or entity that has buying authority and who is the beneficiary of the project deliverable. Customers can be internal or external, individuals or organizations.

cycle time - The time required to complete one cycle of an operation, or to complete a task or function from start to finish.

D

defect - A flaw, shortcoming, or fault. The departure of a quality characteristic from its acceptable level or state.

deliverable - A product or service that can be provided as promised.

delivery window - A specified time, during which a specified quantity of things or services must be delivered to a specified place.

DMAIC - The acronym for the Define, Measure, Analyze, Improve, Control phases in Six Sigma methodology – commonly employed when an organization wishes to improve on an existing process.

downstream - Later stages in the production process.

E

ergonomic - The quality of being functionally designed to minimize the time, effort, and movement required, and to maximize comfort and effectiveness.

error-proofing - Using built-in mechanisms to prevent errors from occurring or to correct them immediately if they do.

F

future state (value stream) map - A graphical and chronological representation of how processes, information, and resources ought to flow in the value stream.

G

Green Belt - Typically full-time employees in an organization who play a vital role in Six Sigma project teams. They operate in support or under the supervision of Black Belts and usually spend about 25% to 30% of their time on Six Sigma projects.

H

Hoshin Kanri - A Lean tools approach to strategic and operational planning involving the systematic analysis, planning, implementation, and reviewing of business processes, with the goals of managing change, developing employee capabilities, and improving performance.

I

inventory - Money or resources tied up in a system in the form of raw material, work-in-progress, and finished goods.

J

jidoka - A Lean strategy involving a standard process to reduce the number of defects produced. Employees and machines detect errors, stop the process, fix the presenting problem, and then investigate the root cause of the problem.

JIT production - See just-in-time production.

just-in-time production - Abbreviated as JIT production, a system in which products are created only once they've been ordered by a customer.

K

kaizen - A Japanese term meaning "improvement." In the Lean philosophy, it refers to the continuous improvement of processes by all employees in an organization.

kaizen event - An application of the Kaizen philosophy, carried out by a cross-functional team, that involves identifying waste and its causes within a specified target area, and implementing Lean solutions to eliminate the waste.

kaizen event charter - A planning document outlining the scope, personnel, and logistics of a Kaizen event.

kanban - A system that makes use of cues – often in the form of cards – to inform employees when a process should be implemented, or when items should be moved to a subsequent step in a production process.

L

lead time - The time taken for a unit to flow through the entire production process.

Lean - A philosophy and set of practices that focus on eliminating waste and creating value, through dynamic, knowledge-driven, and customer-focused strategies.

levelled production - Production in which cycle times have been synchronized so products can flow evenly through the process.

line balancing - A Lean tool that allows you to optimize personnel use so that the workload is equitably distributed.

low-hanging fruit - Problems, inefficiencies, sources of waste, or obstacles to flow that are quick and easy to remedy.

M

muda - A Japanese term meaning waste.

N

non-value- adding activity - A task or process that does not meet the three criteria for a value-adding activity.

O

operator - Any employee who completes a specific task.

P

PDCA cycle - Acronym for plan-do-check-act cycle, a four-step cycle that aims for continual process improvement.

plan-do-check-act cycle - See PDCA cycle.

poka yoke - A Japanese term meaning "mistake-proofing", and referring to mechanisms that automatically detect or correct errors. Also see error-proofing.

process - A set of steps or actions that take a specific input and manipulate it to produce a desired output.

progressive inspection - The standardized inspection each employee carries out on each item before beginning work in a Lean system.

pull production - A production system in which the start of each product assembly process is triggered by the completion of another at the end of a production line, and with products produced only once customers demand them.

push production - A production system in which production is scheduled based on forecasted rather than existing demand for products.

Q

quality - The degree to which a product or service fulfills requirements and conforms to users' expectations.

quality at source - The absence of defects or errors in a unit while it is still going through a process.

R

required value-adding activity - A non-value-adding activity that is required to keep a business running or to meet legal or regulatory requirements.

S

Seiketsu - A Japanese term meaning "standardize." It's the fourth component in the 5S methodology.

Seiton - A Japanese term meaning set in place, which is the second component in the 5S methodology. During this step, tools and items are arranged ergonomically so they can be accessed and used without wasted motion or effort.

Shitsuke - A Japanese term meaning "sustain". It's the fifth component in the 5S methodology, and involves maintaining the improvements realized through the other steps.

Sieri - A Japanese term meaning "sort." It's the first component in the 5S methodology, and involves tidying a workspace and removing unnecessary items.

Sieso - A Japanese term meaning "shine." It's the third component in the 5S methodology, and involves tidying or neatening a work area.

Six Sigma - A process, product, and service improvement approach that aims at removing the causes of defects from processes and by reducing variation in those processes.

source inspection - In a Lean system, the standardized inspection each employee carries out on each item, after completing work on it and before passing it on.

SPC - See statistical process control.

standard operating procedure - A protocol or defined approach for completing a task.

standard work - The specification of a particular order in which different tasks are performed in a given process. These protocols are designed to be as efficient as possible.

standardization - The removal of variation to ensure that things, actions, procedures, or criteria are as close as possible to identical.

statistical process control - Abbreviated as SPC, a mathematically based technique used to monitor production outputs and to provide early warnings of production problems.

statistics - A branch of applied mathematics that provides methods for collecting, analyzing, and interpreting numerical data.

supply chain - The network of suppliers, manufacturers, distributors, transporters, storage facilities, wholesalers, and retailers that participate in the procurement of raw material, production, and delivery of a particular product or service.

T

takt time -A German term meaning "rhythm." In a Lean approach, takt time is the time it must take to produce one product at a rate that keeps up with customer demand.

trigger - Something that initiates a process or event.

V

value - Economic or financial worth. Also, customers' perceptions of the ability of a product or service to satisfy their needs and wants.

value stream - All of the tasks and actions involved in creating and delivering value to customers – for example, through the design, production, and delivery of a product.

value stream map - See VSM.

value stream mapping - A visual representation of all the elements in a value stream. It's useful for identifying and minimizing waste or obstacles that impede the flow of value to customers.

value-add activity - A task or process that fulfills a customer's needs or preferences, changes the product or service in some way, and is done right the first time in the process.

variation - Any item, process, or task that doesn't directly add value for the customer.

Visual Factory - A factory that applies Visual Workplace practices.

Visual Office - An office that applies Visual Workplace practices.

Visual Workplace - A workplace that effectively uses visual cues – such as signs, layouts, charts, and color codes – to convey information.

VSM - Abbreviation of value stream map, a graphic representation of a targeted value stream that shows both material and communication flows.

W

waste - Any item, process, or task that does not directly add value for a customer.

\#

5 Whys - A problem-solving technique that involves asking the question "Why?" at least five times in sequence to identify the root cause of a problem.

5S - A methodology for creating and maintaining a clean and ergonomically ordered work environment. The five components of this methodology are sort, set in order, shine, standardize, and sustain.

www.ingramcontent.com/pod-product-compliance
Lightning Source LLC
Chambersburg PA
CBHW020855180526
45163CB00007B/2516